Taking Up the Timbrel

Taking Up the Timbrel

*The Challenge of Creating Ritual
for Jewish Women Today*

Edited by Sylvia Rothschild
and Sybil Sheridan

SCM PRESS

0 334 02806 x

This edition first published 2000 by
SCM Press
9–17 St Albans Place London N1 0NX

SCM Press is a division of
SCM-Canterbury Press Ltd

Printed in Great Britain by
Biddles Ltd, Guildford and King's Lynn

Contents

Contents

Preface

And Miriam, the Prophetess, the sister of Aaron took up the timbrel in her hand; and all the women went out after her with timbrels and with dances (Exodus 13.20)

A woman, after hours in labour, gives birth. In the moments of relief, gratitude and wonder at the marvellous infant, she wants to give thanks to God. She turns to the prayer book and finds a formal service to take place in the synagogue some time later. There is nothing to capture the moment.

A couple have just been told that their fertility treatment has failed, that they will never have children. If they look at the prayer book they will find prayers for naming a child, for circumcision, for Bar- and perhaps Bat-Mitzvah. A person living alone. The prayers surrounding life-cycle events in the prayer books seem to focus on marriage and the upbringing of children. Where are their life events recorded? Is nothing to be made liturgically of their own hopes and experiences? Without children in Judaism, do women exist?

We are liturgically dumb. The prayer book – a creation of men for specific formal and public worship – only occasionally casts a nod in the direction of women. Until very recently a woman's prayer life was a private affair summed up in the verse of Psalm 45, *k'vod bat melekh p'nimah* – 'the glory of the King's daughter is within'. This has been understood to mean two things. First, that the woman's sphere of life was indoors: at home while her husband presented the public face of the family. Secondly, women's spirituality was seen as internal – without need of the outward trappings of *tallit* or *t'fillin* or any other public display of piety. Women prayed, but at home and alone, and we have little knowledge how much that prayer followed the rules set down by men and how much was extempory, or followed rules drawn up by the women themselves.

The situations described above, of birth, of infertility of the single woman, are not new ones. They are as old as humanity itself. What is different is that today, through the high profile of the women rabbis, the issue is becoming a public one. In the past hundred years, women have penetrated the realm of public prayer. In Progressive Synagogues – in Reform and Liberal Jewish communities – women take their place equally alongside the men. But for some women, praying only the male prayer book has proved to be limiting. They turned to the women rabbis for help, and slowly we have begun to create ritual for those life-cycle events that have no place in standard Jewish practice.

Rituals to mourn the death of an infant are one example. Traditional Judaism does not recognize a child under the age of thirty days as fully viable as a life. This goes back to the days when more babies died than survived, and it was seen as a kindness to parents that no mourning customs should be required. Today, where most children are planned for – longed for – the relationship of the mother to the being in her womb is very different. The expectations are to life, not to death, and so neonatal mortality becomes a terrible blow. Most rabbis are very sympathetic, but this does not change the fact that there is no way in which the parents can properly mourn.

Then there is the intrinsic inequality created by the ceremony of circumcision. The ritual for a boy is not just a medical act, but a ceremony of naming and of entering the covenantal community that began with Abraham. The implication to the modern woman is that girls do not have a part in that covenant and that their name is not of any real religious value. It is time to redress the balance, to reflect in our birth rituals the reality that women have every bit as strong a part to play in the heritage of Israel.

More controversial is the inclusion of ritual following an abortion. Though permitted as a therapeutic act in Judaism, abortion is not to be encouraged, and it does not fit comfortably within the framework of a Jewish liturgy that at all times is dedicated to life. Yet at the moment of decision, and at the moment when the act is performed, a woman needs her God maybe more than at any other time and a ritual can help – not to justify, but to come to terms with what is being done.

The text concerning Miriam raises many questions. After the escape from Egypt and the miraculous parting of the sea, Moses sings a song of triumph. Why does Miriam not sing with him? What words did she sing? Why is she described not as Moses' sister but as Aaron's? And what is a timbrel?

The answer to the first question lies within the text itself. Miriam did not sing with Moses because he sang alone (Exodus 15.1). In contrast, Miriam sings together with the women and not only sings, but accompanies the song with instruments and with dance. Is this a different pattern of worship? Many of the rituals described in this volume depend on highly visual symbols and actions, and there are times when we, like Miriam, are at a loss for words.

The silence that follows Miriam's opening line has received many interpretations. Perhaps she simply echoed Moses' words. Perhaps she did not have the inspiration or ability to complete her song. Or perhaps she disapproved of Moses' description of God as a God of war. Whatever the truth of it, Miriam's silence has become the symbol for all of women's prayers down the ages; prayers that are not recorded, whose contents are unknown. But her opening line has become the symbol for our new-found courage in creating liturgy – to complete the song. It has become the symbol for a women's way of forming prayers; as a collective, and opening up the process as we do here, for others to complete.

Why Miriam is described as Aaron's sister can also be interpreted in this way. It is Aaron, not Moses, who sets down the pattern for future Jewish worship. Aaron began his career as Moses' mouthpiece – it is he who formed the words his brother was unable to say. Later, he became the High Priest, responsible for performing complicated acts of ritual on behalf of the people. Our passage suggests that Miriam may have had a similar role for the women. We have in her a model that many women today unconsciously emulate; she is a 'doer' rather than a 'talker', an 'enabler' rather than a 'leader'.

The American educator Joel Grishaver tells an interesting story regarding the timbrel. The Hebrew is *tof* – a hand-held instrument that was struck like a drum. He asked a class of teenagers the following question. If you were fleeing Egypt for your life, and could only take essentials, would you remember to pack a timbrel? If not, where did the timbrels come from?

> One group of three girls presented a well-worked, carefully rehearsed and reedited collective story . . .
>
> 'They didn't actually have drums with them. But, it was such an emotional experience, and their hearts were beating so loudly that their heartbeats sounded like drums. When they sang, they sang with their hearts.' . . .
>
> One of the boys stood up and said 'Wrong! . . . This is the right answer – I think they were Egyptian [war] drums that floated to the surface.'[1]

The story may appear to present an exaggerated stereotype, but it describes the reality that despite equal opportunities, differences of perception still persist. And if these differences persist, then, by definition the traditional prayers cannot have the same meanings and the same resonances to both sexes.

Thus it becomes important to take a look at traditional rituals to see how women perceive them and ask if they have as much meaning as they should. The classical wedding ceremony harks back to a time when women were 'purchased' as a commodity. How much of our ritual today reflects what we now understand by marriage? Similarly, divorce reflects the 'release' of a woman back into the general pool of singles free for marriage to any man. Is that how we want to mark the end of a relationship?

This book attempts four things. It attempts to understand the process that goes into the creation of new ritual and new liturgy. It attempts to recreate some of the prayer life of bygone ages. It attempts to give new understanding to old liturgy by using prayer and biblical verse in new contexts. And finally, it attempts to create new rituals to cover those many circumstances in life where we yearn for a prayer and find ourselves without one.

The book is not comprehensive. The rituals included reflect the lives of the women rabbis involved. As a group, few of us have yet reached fifty. Thus the main body of ritual concentrates on issues surrounding fertility and infertility. Subjects such as menopause, retirement, different illnesses, welcoming grandchildren, wedding anniversaries, and the many scenarios regarding death are ones we hope to explore in a future volume.

Nor are the rituals just for women. Though they come out of women's experience, many – mourning a beloved pet, moving home or community, struggling with depression, searching for healing – are experiences common to all. Nor are they just for Jews. Though couched in traditional words and using specifically Jewish symbols, the experience of prayer and the use of ritual is a universal one.

Nor are the rituals themselves necessarily complete. Faced with the realization that the general often means the vague, we went for the specific and more potent option. Many rituals were created for just one person and they may not necessarily find resonance with others. But they are there not just to be used, but to be changed. Rituals are repeated, altered, honed over centuries before they become accepted parts of our tradition. Though named here after their creators, they are not the property of the individual rabbis, but belong to all women who choose to make them their own.

This book forms part of a process that will not be completed in our lifetime, but one which we hope will be continued by all who read it, and by the next generation – and by the next.[2]

Women have always prayed, and their prayers have always been deeply personal, deeply moving. *K'vod bat melech p'nimah* – the glory of the King's daughter is within – the source of a woman's prayer is her heartbeat. We are fortunate to live in an age where we can commit these prayers to print and finally take up the challenge of Miriam to sing in our own language and to sing in our own name . . .

לַיהוָה כִּי-גָאֹה גָּאָה

to the Eternal, the one who is greatly exalted.

Creating Ritual

Expanding the Borders of Prayer

Sylvia Rothschild

As a young student rabbi I was confronted with the prayer with which we begin the majority of our services, the *Mah Tovu*, and was asked to translate it. All went well until I came across a line taken from the book of Psalms (69.14), '*Va'ani t'fillati l'kha Adonai eit ratzon*'. I responded by using the translation I had seen all my life: 'And as for me, may my prayer come before you God at the proper time.' 'No,' said my teacher, 'look at it again.' I tried again. Then the penny dropped: the Hebrew is constructed in an unusual and challenging way. It reads, 'And as for me, I am a prayer before you God at the proper time.' It changed my view of liturgy for ever – not the 'prayer' but the 'pray-er' is the focus and the conduit for meaningful connection with God; not the words of the text but the conversation of the heart. Everything else is vanity.

Prayer is deeply personal. At its best it addresses the feelings and needs of the individual who is praying. It crystallizes them and reorders them, providing a context in which the pray-er can grow, a space within which the connection with God can emerge. Rather like the best Torah study, bringing yourself, your own perspectives, your own experiences to the text means that you and it live in a different way. You deepen yourself, add layers of insight and understanding, enable yourself to live your life in a richer and more complex universe. By expressing the self in prayer, by becoming a prayer, the religious human being fulfils her or his spiritual search.

Entering the congregational rabbinate often feels like a form of prayer in action. Chameleon-like, you enter the lives and feelings of your congregation, often acting as the representative of a tradition they want and need but feel distanced from. When something happens to them or their families, they want the rabbi. They need a ceremony or a text within which they can identify and share with their community the experience they are undergoing. Even today, maybe especially today, when the bonds of traditional daily religious practice are loosening, people look for religious language to express the important events in their lives; they look for liturgy and they look for ritual.

Congregational rabbis are constantly being faced with the need for a Jewish way to mark a life-cycle event, a turning point or crisis, a spiritual peak or trough. The pastoral rabbi serves the community not only by offering legal pronouncements, or by teaching texts or preaching theology, but also by creating the opportunity for prayer to become real. We work in a world where many life experiences are invisible to our liturgy, and where our traditional liturgy and ritual is often out of touch with the people for whom it is intended. Starting where the people are, we find a large and uncharted world of barely expressed religious need, a sort of *tohu va'vohu*[1] of human emotion and yearning, for which the response has to be the immediate and careful creation of ceremonial and prayer texts, so that we enable our people to become, in the words of our own services, their own prayers. The task is very clear: the problem is not the 'what?' nor the 'why?' – it is the 'how?'.

How do we create new rituals and liturgies? And how do we make what we create impeccably Jewish? Most of the religious expressions that we use today have been built up over many generations, refined and polished by the experiences and the concentrated use of Jewish pray-ers. They have acquired something of the beauty and patina of well-loved antique furniture, which somehow fits into whatever situation it finds itself in. The emotion has been felt in the heat of the moment and also recollected in tranquillity time and time again. There is a smoothness and a flow, a sense of inevitability in the rhythms, of *'eit ratzon'* – a fittingness. To develop new words and practices ready for our communities sometimes feels rather like creating atonal loud brashness in a hushed concert hall. But prayer has to be relevant if it is to live and have meaning, and the pray-er must feel the immediacy and excitement of that life.

So in creating words and actions for modern life-events one must be prepared to break out of the recognized forms and phrases where necessary and try other symbols, other methods of exploring and sharing and expressing, for example using movement and dance. That said, there are components of Jewish prayer and liturgy which one can analyse and replicate, albeit in new forms or with new words.

It seems to me that the three most basic components of Jewish prayer are: that it is most powerfully done within the context of a community; that there are rhythms which place you in the world, then draw you in to a special liminal space, and finally bring you safely to rest back in the world in your new state; and that Jewish prayer almost always operates along a spectrum of tension between two states – for example the universal with the particular, the immanent with the trans-cendent, the creation with the revelation. With these roots of people and place, of direction and transformation, and of the boundaries held in place with a creative tension, the pray-ers are able to express their emotion safely within a religious context, and transform the experience into genuine and life-enhancing prayer. They can pierce the very heavens, and pene-trate the most experience-hardened human heart.

To begin with, when developing new liturgy or ritual, one must create the awareness of community and of place. For any prayer or ritual to have meaning, it must operate with the active co-operation of people who have come for a known reason, who are focussed on explicitly stating that reason, and who are able and willing to work together in the presence of God. In the first instance I often find myself looking for selections of psalms or sung texts to facilitate this. Better than many more modern prayers, the verses of the psalms address the reality of life and provide a comforting stream of familiar words on which to float and navigate the newer prayer. *B'rakhot*, with their well-known *p'tihah*, the formula embedded in our Jewish minds since infancy, may also serve this purpose. To state within the blessing protocol the purpose of our being together is to set the agenda in a gentle and specific way. We focus on the nature and attributes of God before we move into our own situation. A psalm or sung text, a blessing, a specially written prayer – all set the scene and allow a group of people to come together. An act such as lighting a candle or ceremonially bringing in an object or a person (think of *huppah* or of the ceremony of *b'rit milah*) may also focus the ritual. An object close to the focus of the ritual – a certificate of birth or death or divorce, a favourite item associated with the lost person or a symbol of status – such things can clarify the point from which we are departing, and when we return to them changed by our experience, the change may also be seen in the way we view such inanimate objects.

Having created a sense of time and space, having built a community working together to pray through an experience or situation, it is time to focus on the rhythms which will draw the participants from the mundane world into liminal and transformational space, and then return them anew to the safety of the day-to-day realm.

This centrepiece of any ritual and liturgy is the most problematic, and requires enormous sensitivity to the needs and the spiritual language of the participants for whom it is created. There must be words or actions which speak the prayer. The participants must be allowed to be active in the process – by speaking their own words, by the movements of their bodies, by handling a relevant object. Here, more than anywhere, the notion of pray-er as prayer must be fostered and nourished. Here permission can be given for the connection with God at whatever level the pray-er is capable of achieving. One way to do this is to create a bounded space for meditation. A *niggun*, a wordless prayer bound up in repeating a gently insistent tune, is often able to do this. The singer holds the space while the pray-er prays, and the participants join in as and when they are able to do so.

Sometimes pray-ers may share their experiences in real time.

Sometimes the others may breathe words of encouragement, or share their own prayer, sometimes the textured quality of deepening meditation may cover the whole experience. One should plan for activity, even if it is to be abandoned in favour of the prayerful silence. If one knows that there are words there to be said, even if they don't fully express the moment, then there is a sense of safety and a knowledge that the whole event is being held within a structure. Here again the book of Psalms comes into its own. Wherever we look within this poetry, we are aware that we are following in the footsteps of the pray-er *par excellence* that, as Kohelet has said, there is nothing new under the sun.

It may be that a single action can express the centre of the prayer. The symbolic opening or closing of a door, the act of transferring something from one place to another – to move a wedding ring to another finger, to tear up a document, to place a treasured photograph inside a frequently used *siddur*, to plant a tree, to light one candle from another – the list is end-less. Whatever is done, it must be both symbolically appro-priate and explicit. It must be seen to be done and the action must be seen to begin and end. There is time for song and for silence, for words and for touch, all of which will lead the pray-er further in, hold her or his expressed will, and gently but firmly guide her or him through and back towards the world. Time to pray is essential, as is structure and the sense of the whole edifice having been thought through and being held by those participating in it. It is important, too, to talk about what has been done, to talk the journey through, and to bring that journey to an end, rooted back in the extraordinarily ordi-nary experience of sharing with people who care. Think of our current rituals: the shaking of the seated mourner's hand after a funeral, the moment of emergence at the end of *yihud* at a wedding, the convivial *kiddush* after each service in the synagogue. We need those moments of meeting together to root ourselves back in our world. To leave someone stranded on a spiritual high or low is to betray them.

The third ingredient of Jewish prayer and liturgy is the

creative tension found in so many of our traditions, where two states co-exist simultaneously in our hearts and minds. For example, we celebrate at Pesah with bread that is both the bread of affliction and the bread of liberation; we celebrate our fragility and dependence on God at Sukkot with the bringing in of the first fruits. Our prayer books are filled with wondrous paradoxes – praising the true Judge when faced with the death of someone we care for, lighting Shabbat candles with the blessing 'Who commands us to light the Shabbat lights' despite the biblical prohibition against light being seen in our houses on shabbat,[2] so that we generate a sense of religious warmth and closeness even while apparently breaking a biblical command. The very best insight and Jewish scholarship has traditionally emerged from the work around ideas which cannot exist together and yet which we know do precisely that. The Talmudic process is predicated on understanding and harmonizing opposing propositions. Jewish prayer is no different from Jewish scholarship: it thrives on the interface between the two states – universal and particular, transcendent and immanent, personal and communal, heart and mind . . .

In particular, Jewish prayer is built on the two places of our meeting with God – what one might call the state of Creation and the state of Exodus/Revelation. Creation encompasses God as universal Creator, master of the Universe, transcendent Being. Exodus/Revelation speaks to us as children of the Covenant in our particular relationship with God of mutual obligation and interdependence. We move between these two places constantly, sometimes in paragraphs within the same prayer (for example the *Aleinu* prayer), at other times within the time-frame of the day (for instance the preamble to *kiddush* on Friday night which talks about the seventh day of creation, and the one on Saturday morning which reminds us to keep the covenant of which Shabbat is a sign).

When one writes prayers or chooses symbols or rituals to express moments in a life that need a formal religious rite, it is important to keep in mind both of these states, to use them to create the dynamic and the journey both into the central moment and then back out into the world. Some things fall obviously into one category or the other, but most are a mixture of the two, as they express both a current state and a need to move on. We talk about the dead being bound up *bitzrur hahayyim* – in the ropes of life – and it seems to me that these ropes are created from a blend of Creation and Exodus, of particular and general, of what is and what could be.

Liturgy and ritual are being created by congregational rabbis all the time, be it a new *mi she-beirakh* for a special occasion, or an innovative service for entering an old-age home. There is no recipe for making unfailingly good liturgy, no guarantee that what is created will last for longer than the moment for which it was designed. We are in the business of enabling people to be their own prayers, of returning people to the tradition of weaving their own words around generally agreed themes and structure. Generalizable liturgy by its very nature will be more anodyne and dilute than a bespoke tailor-made ceremony, but there is great value in having access to a library of other people's prayers, other people's ideas, symbols and rituals. This is, after all, the origin of the *siddur*.

We begin the majority of our services with a quotation from Psalm 69 which reminds us that we are all our own prayers, that we hope to come before God at a time that is *ratzon* – desirable, appropriate and proper – and also that we hope for God, in abundant mercy, to answer us in such a way that we are able to make the transition from distress to liberation. It is a huge agenda to set ourselves – and God – and yet we regularly do so. Jewish prayer emerges from Jewish experience. It is rooted in our perceptions of Covenant and of Creation, it bridges the liminal space between then and now, between reality and potential, between traditional construction and contemporary understanding. It moves us on, and it must move with us.

Women, Prayer and Ritual in the Bible

Rachel Montagu

What is the significance of prayer in religion? It is one of the fundamental religious acts. To converse with God is one of the essential roles of the soul. How does the Bible describe prayer? Because of the importance in the development of Jewish liturgy of Hannah's prayer asking to conceive her son Samuel, this is an area where women's contribution is significant in our tradition, although of course many of the experiences of prayer recorded in the Bible, and certainly the first uses of the word, are masculine ones.

What is prayer? In English it is defined by the dictionary as 'making devout supplication to God, beseeching'.[1] The Hebrew word *lehitpallel* is reflexive and means not only asking and interceding but also judging;[2] prayer in the Hebrew language is not just about reaching out to the Almighty but about influencing oneself, judging oneself by that reaching out.

We see in Genesis 4.26 that prayer is something human beings learned in the course of time after the creation, rather than being an immediate instinct of God's created beings:

To Seth also a son was born, and [Adam] named him Enosh. At that time people began to invoke the name of the Eternal.

Later comes a warning that intense closeness to God can make it impossible to continue to live in this human world:

Enoch walked with God; then he was not, because God took him (Gen. 5.24).

The standard English sense of 'prayer' is a request. When Abraham and Sarah go to Gerar, Abraham pretends that Sarah is his sister lest the natives kill him in order to take her.[3] King Abimelech is told in a dream that he will be punished for taking a married woman:

> Now then, return the man's wife; for he is a prophet, and he will pray for you and you shall live (Genesis 20.7).

At the beginning of the Books of Samuel, we have another example of a prayer requesting something. Hannah prayed to God for a child – perhaps she prayed, not her husband Elkanah because he was happy with the *status quo*. Elkanah had two wives, Peninah who had children and Hannah who did not. We are told that year after year they went on pilgrimage to sacrifice at the shrine at Shiloh. As was customary, they left part of the sacrifice at the shrine and ate part themselves. Elkanah gave single portions to Peninah and her children but a double portion to Hannah because he loved her. When Hannah wept in distress at Peninah's taunts at her childlessness, he asked her whether he was not more to her than ten sons. We can assume that Elkanah enjoyed having a family provided by one wife, while another wife had nothing to distract her from focussing all her love and maternal energy on him, but clearly neither of his wives was satisfied. If Peninah was content she would not have tried to distress Hannah; if Hannah was happy, then Peninah's jibes could not have reduced her to tears.

After they had all feasted on their portions, Hannah returned to the shrine and wept and prayed. When she was challenged and accused of being drunk by Eli the high priest, who had seen her standing and soundlessly moving her lips, she replied:

> I have drunk neither wine nor spirits but I have been pouring out my soul before the Eternal . . . I have been speaking out of my great anxiety and vexation all this time.

We cannot tell to what extent prayers as well as sacrifices were routinely offered in the shrine: Eli's surprise suggests that prayer was unusual there. Hannah's 'pouring out my soul' has become one of the paradigms of all Jewish prayer. A mediaeval midrash equates Hannah's prayer with the *T'fillah*, the prayer said three times daily in which Jews praise God, thank God and ask for all life's blessings, especially redemption: the rabbis decreed that saying the *T'fillah* replaced the Temple offerings as service to God once the Temple was destroyed, leaving the Jewish community bereft of their accustomed form of divine worship.[4]

Once Hannah had received Eli's assurance that her prayer was acceptable to God, she felt able to rejoin her family and feast with them.

Once her prayers had come to fruition, she fulfilled the vow she made in her prayer and brought her son Samuel back to the shrine and sang a song of joy to God. A major theme of her song is that God can change things and allow the oppressed to triumph. The midrashic suggestion that her original prayer was the *T'fillah* is completely anachronistic because this prayer was developed later, in the rabbinic period, but there are a number of common themes in the *T'fillah* and her song; praising God, God's power over life and death, the need for sustenance for the hungry, the importance of knowledge.

It is from Hannah's private outpourings of the heart that Jewish law derives the physical position in which the *T'fillah*, the structured formal prayer, is said: standing facing towards the Temple in Jerusalem, lips moving but no sound audible to others – or only just. And of course not drunk. So the key prayer of modern Jewish liturgy, often incorrectly regarded as a rather male preserve,[5] is happily associated by the mediaeval rabbis with a woman's prayer, perhaps the best-detailed example in the Bible of trust in God's willingness to respond to a human cry for help.

Rebecca is the first matriarch from whom we learn a reason for speaking to God. The matriarchs have difficulty fulfilling their eponymous role and producing children to inherit God's covenant. Rebecca was barren; Isaac prayed for her and she conceived. Why was it Isaac who prayed for her when Rebecca was obviously not shy to address God herself? When she had become pregnant and then felt within her body the beginnings of her twin sons' near-lifetime of battle and found their struggles too painful, she went to ask God what was happening to her (Genesis 25.20–23). The Hebrew word used is *lidrosh*, which means to search out: just as the mediaeval rabbinic midrash searched for meaning within the texts, so Rebecca applied to God for an explanation.

The midrash seems more willing than the Bible to value the prayers of women and says that Rachel became pregnant not because of a husband's intercession, like Rebecca, but because all four of Jacob's wives prayed together for her to have a child.

An extraordinary reason for the matriarchs' difficulties in child-bearing is suggested in the midrash on Song of Songs:

> Why were the matriarchs so long barren? Because the Holy One longed to hear their prayer. God said to them: 'My dove, I will tell you why I have kept you childless; because I was longing to hear your prayer.' Hence it says, For sweet is your voice and your countenance is comely.[6]

This is one of those texts which it is hard to know how to inter-pret correctly. Do we take it as a text which proves God's long-ing for communication and a rabbinic validation of women's prayer to God, or do we take it as proof of a capricious God who puts human beings through tests of faith, however trying, as in the stories of the suffering of Job and the binding of Isaac?

One of the dilemmas of a Bible reader is whether Hagar, Bilhah and Zilpah, who bear children to the patriarchs, should be regarded as matriarchs or not. Is it social snobbery to exclude the slave women? Is it ridiculous to include in the covenant with God women who seem not to have any link with their Creator? While Zilpah and Bilhah have no voice within the biblical text, we hear more of Hagar's conversation with

God and visions of God than those of Sarah, Rebecca, Rachel or Leah. Hagar was the first woman to bear a son for God's covenant. However, her communication with God illustrates the ambivalence we noted earlier about women's conversations with God. When Abraham obeyed Sarah's command to send Ishmael and Hagar out into the desert and the two of them were alone and thirsty, Hagar wept and spoke, yet God's answer is described as a response to Ishmael, whose voice the reader has not heard (Genesis 21.9–21). Earlier Hagar had encountered an angel the first time Sarah sent her away, before Ishmael's birth; then, in a spirit of grateful astonishment, she named God and the well where she met the angel:

> So [Hagar] named the Eternal who spoke to her, You are *El-ro-i*; for she said, 'Have I really seen God and remained alive after seeing him?' Therefore the well was called *Be'er-lahai-ro-i*; it lies between Kadesh and Bered (Genesis 16.13–14).

It is to *Be'er-lahai-ro-i* that Isaac goes after Abraham bound him for sacrifice and then God rejected his willingness to die. Perhaps he hoped that visiting the place where Hagar encountered an angel would enable him to share Hagar's sense of nearness to God and enable him to understand what had happened on Mount Moriah, why God had first asked his father to sacrifice him and then, when he consented to die, suddenly refused to accept his self-offering. One can understand why Abraham had to send his servant to find Isaac a wife; he was too disorientated and demoralized at that time to look for one himself. It is near Hagar's well that he and Rebecca meet on her journey to Canaan with Abraham's servant and Isaac then takes her to his mother's tent (Genesis 24.67).

The Bible carefully links Sarah, Rebecca and their tent. Penina Adelman has suggested that the link is not only the personal one generated by Isaac's needs and love; the matriarch's connection to God became the paradigm for the

Temple, the place where the whole Jewish people sought access
to God. In their tent the matriarchs welcomed God's presence,
kept a light always burning, offered hospitality and always had
bread as a visible sign of God's blessing for those with whom
a covenant had been made; all these things were important
features of the later tent of meeting in the wilderness.

> Then Isaac brought her into his mother Sarah's tent. He
> took Rebecca, and she became his wife; and he loved her. So
> Isaac was comforted after his mother's death (Genesis
> 24.67).

> Midrash Rabbah: You find that as long as Sarah lived, a
> cloud hung over her tent; when she died, that cloud dis-
> appeared; but when Rebecca came, it returned. As long as
> Sarah lived, her doors were wide open; at her death that
> liberality ceased; but when Rebecca came, that open-
> handedness returned. As long as Sarah lived, there was a
> blessing on her dough, and the lamp used to burn from the
> evening of the Sabbath until the evening of the following
> Sabbath; when she died, these ceased, but when Rebecca
> came, they returned.[7]

While Jewish liturgy addresses prayers to the God of Abraham,
Isaac and Jacob and quotes the biblical prayers of David and
Solomon, the *tehines*, prayers written in Yiddish for women
which cover the same occasions as the standard liturgy and
also those events in women's lives ignored by traditional
prayer books such as pregnancy, birth and feeding a child,
often speak to the God of the matriarchs or other female
figures of the Bible, especially where some event in the life of
the biblical woman referred to is relevant. This gives biblical
women the same status as role models for prayer for their
female descendants that their male equivalents have for Jewish
men.[8] While there are no examples of a biblical woman blessing her daughters or grand-daughters that compare with Jacob
blessing his grandsons, Ephraim and Menasseh, all Jewish girls

are blessed each Friday night with the words 'May you be like Sarah, Rebecca, Rachel and Leah.'

There are some figures in the Bible who tantalize us because so little is said about them, and yet they are clearly of great importance. One of these is Miriam, described in the book of Exodus as a prophet and by Micah as equal to her brothers Aaron and Moses.[9] We have only a verse or two of her song of praise to God for rescuing the people at the Red Sea,[10] while we have the whole text of the song of her brother Moses. It was Moses, not Miriam, who prayed 'God, please heal her' when she contracted leprosy and was barred from the camp (Exodus 15.20–21; Numbers 12.1–13).

Miriam's song at the Red Sea is not the only example of women publicly singing a prayer of thanksgiving. Deborah, prophet and 'mother in Israel', sang to God after defeating the Canaanites. In this long and triumphant poem the milk of the prose account of Jael's hospitality to Sisera becomes transmuted into the more memorable 'curds in a lordly dish'.

Sybil Sheridan suggests that it is possible that both the Song of Songs and Lamentations represent a tradition of women composers and performers of wedding and mourning songs.[11] Miriam's song, Deborah's song and position as a judge and the women's role as singers at weddings and funerals all make it clear that despite the lack of detailed information available to us, women had a public role in communal life and worship in biblical times.

Another example of women gathering for a ritual is Jepthah's daughter's request for two months to bewail her virginity on the mountains with her companions before Jepthah kills her, carrying out his foolish vow to sacrifice the first creature to come out to meet him when he returned to his home after the battle if God gave him victory.[12] We are told that this became an annual four-day ritual for the daughters of Israel, but not what exactly they said or did as part of their commemorations.

There are other shared rituals of the daughters of Israel cited in the Bible which are more difficult for us to read as the heiresses of the Judaism defined as 'ethical monotheism'. How

are we to view rituals which seem to be more linked to pagan-
ism and yet may be a biblical link to the explicitly feminine
aspects of Godhead which we search for today? We cannot
know what our biblical ancestors meant by names like *Elohim*,
El Shaddai and the Tetragrammaton.[13] We are wholly at home
with our present theology, in which these names and others all
represent the one Eternal and Transcendent God; we ignore
archaeological evidence which suggests that originally they
may have been used for local pagan gods and goddesses and
gradually assimilated into something more like our own concept of deity; for instance El was worshipped jointly with
Asherah.[14] The Bible makes it clear that Jeremiah disapproved
totally of the women who baked cakes for the queen of heaven
(Jeremiah 7.18; 44.17–25),[15] but we cannot know what the
difference there would have been in the eyes of the women of
Jeremiah's time between shewbread for the Eternal and cakes
for the queen of heaven.

Women in the Bible pray to God, seek explanations from
God, sing in praise to God, giving us explicit role models as we
do those things today. The mediaeval rabbis who denied
women an equal role in synagogue liturgy respected the
women's spirituality portrayed in the Bible; they were happy to
state that Hannah prayed the *T'fillah*, even if not happy to let
their wives devote time to prayer which might have been spent
on succouring themselves.[16] As women we can be glad to find
our spirituality can connect to the spirituality of the Bible. But
we cannot fool ourselves that the relationships between
women and God described in the Bible are described in as
much detail or regarded as equally significant to those of men.
Miriam and Moses may be of equal importance in our eyes,
but Miriam's voice does not come from the pages of the
Bible with the resonant authority commanded by her younger
brother. Yet we must recognize, as our tradition has always
done, that the Bible teaches that both men and women are
made in God's image and it is an instinct for all human beings,
male and female, to perform rituals and speak to our Creator.

Discovering Hannah: Women's Rituals in Second-Century Palestine

Sybil Sheridan

The Hannah of the Bible is of great significance in Judaism. The mother of Samuel, whose barrenness caused her to pray with such fervour in the Temple,[1] became in Rabbinic Judaism the model of how to pray.

> Rav Hamnuna said, How many important laws can be derived from these verses relating to Hannah!
>
> 'And Hannah, she spoke in her heart.' From this we learn that in prayer one must pray from the heart.
>
> 'Only her lips moved.' From this we learn that one must form the words with one's lips.
>
> 'But her voice was not heard.' From this we learn that it is forbidden to raise one's voice when praying.[2]

So, to this day, in traditional communities the recitation of the *T'fillah* – the central prayer of Judaism – is said silently, with lips moving and in a state of extreme concentration

But Hannah as the model for perfect prayer is a model that men aspired to. Women's obligations in prayer were hazier and less obligatory. For women Hannah stood for something else – something more. For prayer, yes – but also for ritual . . . and a whole different life-style.

In the Middle Ages, the name Hannah stood as an acronym for the three so-called 'women's *mitzvot*' or commandments. They were: *Hallah* – the separation of the dough of the Sabbath loaf; *Niddah* – the laws relating to menstruation; *Hadlakat ha-ner* – the lighting of the Sabbath lamp.[3] They are first mentioned together in the Mishnah in the following passage:

> For three violations women die in childbirth: for failing to attend to the laws of *niddah*, of *hallah* and of *hadlakat ha-ner*.[4]

The passage is odd – and not just because of the dire nature of the punishment. It is odd that there is a punishment at all. Most laws in the Mishnah are simply stated:

> 'You do this . . . you do that.'

This passage sounds more like the biblical conditional commandments.

> 'If you do this . . . then that will happen.'

Moreover rabbinic punishments tend to be administered by the *Beit Din* – the judicial court. Acts of God as punishment do occur, but never elsewhere is death in childbirth seen as one. Altogether, this passage seems to be one not of law, but of story – a story which we will now attempt to unravel.

But there is a further puzzle in the text. The three laws in this Mishnah are not in fact laws that relate to women. The law of Hallah derives from Numbers 15.19–21, which demands that when eating the produce of the land of Israel, a portion should be set aside as *t'rumah*, a freewill offering to God. Thus any person making bread, the baker as well as the housewife, male as well as female, was bound by that law. The laws of *niddah* go back to the Torah, where in the book of Leviticus (15.19ff.) a woman is charged to separate herself from her husband and touch no one during her menstrual period. Afterwards she must immerse herself in flowing water – a mikveh or a stream – before resuming her normal life. The purpose, in the context of the Torah, was clearly one of ritual purity. No man having touched a menstruating woman could participate in Temple or

Tabernacle worship. Thus, one can argue, the law was there for the sake of the men, not for the women.[5] The law regarding *hadlakat ha-ner* does not come from Torah. It is cited in the Mishnah (Shabbat 2.1) and relates to the lighting of a lamp in the home shortly before sundown on the eve of Shabbat to ensure that there would be light there once Shabbat had started. This was also not originally exclusive to women.

And another puzzle. There is a Mishnaic ruling that states that women are exempted from any positive commandment that must be done at a particular time.[6] Yet these are all positive time-bound commandments and women appear obliged to do them on pain of death! So why should three seemingly random commandments not exclusive to one particular gender become so important to the women of subsequent generations?

To find a possible answer, we have look at the text, not as one written by men looking 'out' into the world of women, but rather as a woman's text that somehow got 'in'.

Niddah. The laws of *niddah* are set in the Bible amongst those of male semen discharge and certain illnesses which prevented a man from entering the Tabernacle precincts. Once there was no Temple, the laws relating to these were no longer necessary. So men ceased ritual immersion, just as they ceased sacrificing, blowing silver trumpets, or doing other things that had been required as part of Temple worship. A principle was established that whatever activities related to the Temple should not be observed when there was no Temple.

But the women kept on observing *niddah* despite the fact that ritually it was no longer necessary. One reason is obvious – it gave them space. A man was forbidden to sleep with his wife during her period and for some days after until she had immersed herself in a mikveh. It meant a woman was not constantly at the beck and call of her husband; it meant their relationship was not based entirely on sex; it meant that women were in control.

But there may be more to it than this. The rabbis required that laws relating to the Temple were to be left in abeyance while no Temple existed, yet the women appear here to be flouting the rule. They deliberately continued to observe a Temple law that was now no longer necessary.

Hallah. Once the Temple was destroyed, the requirement of this offering ceased, along with all other sacrifices. Yet the women continued to put aside a portion of the *hallah* they baked for Shabbat. They could no longer offer it up in the Temple so they burnt it in what looks like a surrogate sacrificial offering. Once again, they seem to be flouting the rabbinic principle regarding observance once the Temple had been destroyed.

Hadlakat ha-ner. This, being a rabbinic rather than biblical law, reflects an age where the Temple was no longer important. The lighting of the Sabbath lamp was very practical and necessary, yet there seems evidence that for the woman the act had much greater significance. *The m'norah* – the seven-branched golden candlestick that stood in the Temple – was lit, by the High Priest[7] each evening at dusk. If the women were intent on preserving aspects of Temple ritual, then to associate their lamp-lighting with the *m'norah* becomes a logical step.

Certainly, by the Middle Ages the entire Sabbath meal was seen as symbolizing the Temple sacrifice. A white tablecloth, two candles, wine, *hallah* and salt all call to mind the ancient ritual, and the woman who prepared the meal, arranged the table and 'declared the Sabbath' by lighting the candles became for that moment *in loco* High Priest.

Thus it was possible for the eighteenth-century Sarah bat Tovim to say after the blessing over the Sabbath candles,

> My *mitzvah* of candle lighting should be accepted as the equivalent of the High Priest lighting the candles in the Temple.[8]

When we take these *mitzvot* together, three observations can be made.

They are strong on ritual. Each one relies on a symbolic gesture using powerful elements: fire and water. What they meant to the second-century Jewish woman can only be guessed at. Destruction and regeneration? Sacrifice and birth? Is there a connection here with the threat of death in childbirth? What we can be sure of is that they were not passive or neutral symbols.

They are weak on liturgy. Words are almost entirely absent. We have today the standard blessings that are said on lighting the candles which are rabbinic in origin. Is the absence of any other words indicative that these *mitzvot* were performed in silence? Evidence of late mediaeval and contemporary prayers suggests not. On the contrary, it was customary for prayers to be said at these important times. But these prayers were either extemporary or handed down orally. The supplications of women were very different from the male ones that make up the standard liturgy.

Thirdly, each commandment seems to preserve an aspect of Temple worship that the men had abandoned. We see in *hallah*, *niddah* and *hadlakat ha-ner* acts of sacrifice, of purification and of dedication.

Finally, let us look at the punishment. Women were, in second-century Palestine, outside the judicial process. Only men became rabbis, only men became judges in the *Beit Din*. Women were not usually accepted as witnesses in legal cases.[9] It would seem likely therefore that legal cases were by definition ones of which the men were aware – ones that impinged on their lives in some way. Women's social lives were so separate from those of men that it is likely that many incidents would pass unnoticed by their husbands and would be resolved by the women themselves. What the process of 'law' would be in these cases is unknown to us, but if we take our text as evidence of women's lives, we see that they call on God to mete out punishment. A woman's experience would have centred upon childbirth. For women married at the age of puberty with little contraception and minimal medical care, maternal death must have been an ever-present fear, a very real possibility –

and for those living their lives under the watchful eye of the Divine it was viewed very logically as a punishment.

Only two women are recorded in the Bible as dying in childbirth. They are Rachel, who died giving birth to Benjamin,[10] and the unnamed wife of Pinhas the son of Eli the priest, who gave birth prematurely on hearing of the capture of the Ark and the death of her husband and father-in-law.[11] Both named their children before they died. Rachel, whose name for her son, Ben-Oni – son of my ordeal – was quickly jettisoned by Jacob, may have been making reference to the punishment given to Eve as well as her own very great pain. The other woman, we are told, named her son 'Ichabod', described as meaning 'the glory has departed from Israel', because the Ark had been captured and taken away by the Philistines.

For the Mishnaic women this last passage may have been significant, for it exactly mirrored their own experience where the spoils of the Temple were taken away by the Romans on their defeat of the Jews in 70 CE.[12] If the purpose of the women's absolute observance of the 'Hannah' *mitzvot* was to preserve key elements of the Temple ritual, then their failure to do them would be to see the 'glory depart from Israel' yet again and their punishment therefore justly deserved. Thus the threat of maternal mortality could be explained as deriving not only from experience, but also from a theological interpretation of a biblical verse.

What our Mishnah passage indicates is that the women of the second century were not religious illiterates, as they are often portrayed. It suggests a very careful and very independent response on their part to the trauma of the times. It suggests that women did not feel themselves bound by the principles that governed rabbinic Judaism, but that they had an autonomy of thought and action which they did not hesitate to exercise. It suggests they were well-educated and sufficiently confident in their education to form their own opinions. All in all, it presents a very different picture of Jewish women from the one we are often led to believe.

Thus we can break the myth of women leaving the religious

life to the men while they got on with the cooking. We have here evidence of a deeply spiritual and theologically articulate community who felt no need to 'break into' the men's world – not because they were satisfied with their domestic role, but because they were satisfied with their religious one. Over the centuries this self-confidence has been eroded, and with the breakdown of the oral tradition most of the ceremonies that made up women's religious life have been lost.[13]

But we have here something that we Jewish women at the beginning of another new era would do well to emulate. We have once more the education and we have again the confidence. All we must do now is create the new rituals and present the new interpretations so that we make new traditions of our own. Then in our turn we may inspire other women in future ages, just as Hannah was the source of inspiration, for so many generations in so many different ways, from her day up to ours.

Rituals of Home and Person

Meditations for *Tallit* and *T'fillin*

Elizabeth Tikvah Sarah

These meditations reflect my personal experience, articulate critical moments in my life. I offer them as an invitation to all who wrap themselves in a *tallit* and/or lay *t'fillin* to write their own meditations expressing the meanings these rituals have for them. Like the tradition of the women's *tehines* of Eastern Europe, which include an array of private prayers related to every aspect of women's domestic lives, the participation of women in Jewish religious life today provides an opportunity for each one of us to make the different rituals we engage in speak in our own language and resonate with the beat of our own lives.

Meditation for *Tallit*

I was wrapped in
fear and
loneliness
for many years
waiting
longing
to be
unwrapped by
love and
fierce-desire
to be
enveloped by
tender-care
forevermore
But then

I got what I wanted
again and again and
lost myself
    unwrapped and
    unravelled
    enveloped and
    enclosed

So now
shattered-scattered
I stand
broken
before You
so now
awed
alone
gathering together the
pieces of
myself
I prepare to
wrap myself
embrace myself
Your sheltering
Presence
hovering around me
beckoning me
trembling me
into life
once more

Blessed are You, our Living God, Sovereign-Presence of the Universe, whose commandments make us holy and who commands us to wrap ourselves in *tzitzit*.

Meditation for *T'fillin*

I cannot
bind myself
to You
I can only
unbind myself
continually and
free
Your spirit
within me
So why
this tender-cruel
parody of
bondage
   black
   leather
   straps
   skin
   gut and
   sacred litany of
     power and
     submission
which binds us
Your slave-people
still?
My own answer is
wound around
with every
taut
binding and
unbinding
blood rushing
heart pounding
life-force surging
   pushing
   panting

straining
struggling to
break through
to You

Blessed are You, Our Living God, Sovereign-Presence of the
Universe, whose commandments make us holy and who
commands us to lay *t'fillin*.

Meditations and Prayers for Use in the *Mikveh*

Alexandra Wright

The *mikveh* is a 'gathering of waters' from a natural source, sufficient in quantity for individuals to immerse themselves. Modern *mikva'ot* use water from a natural source, replenished by water from an invalid source. The *halakhic* regulations are met through the use of technology, though archaeological remains of the Second Temple period show evidence that the modern *mikveh* has remained faithful to its model in the time of the Mishnah and Talmud.

In biblical and rabbinic times, immersion rendered the individual ritually clean. Rules of purity were very strict, not for hygienic or health reasons – for ritual immersion is not about cleansing from physical uncleanness, but for moral or religious purposes. Certain objects or biological conditions, such as menstruation, when perceived through a religious lens, were seen to be spiritually polluting. And only a period of time, followed by a ritual – such as immersion – could render that object fit for use again, or allow individuals to take their place in the full social order, rather than exist on the margins of the community.

The *mikveh* today is used specifically at the conclusion of a woman's period of menstruation and for individuals converting to Judaism. It is important to emphasize that ritual immersion for the convert is not a purification ritual, for that would invalidate or at least deprecate the life and family upbringing of that individual before conversion. The *mikveh* is a symbol of a new chapter in a person's life. It is a threshold, as a person moves from the uncertain and rather unclear boundaries at the

edge of the Jewish community to becoming a fully-fledged and
identified member of that community.

These prayers have been written specifically for the person
converting to Judaism. The *mikveh* is visited immediately
after the individual's interview at the *Beit Din* where one is
often questioned on the knowledge gained during the course
of preparation. Immersion can be a powerful spiritual and
emotional moment at the conclusion of the process of preparation for becoming Jewish.

The first prayer is provided for a quiet moment of meditation and concentration (*kavannah*) before stepping into the
mikveh. The second prayer should be recited by the rabbi or a
friend who welcomes the convert once she has immersed in the
waters.

To be recited by the convert before entering the mikveh:

Eternal God, behold I am about to fulfil the commandment of
t'villah. I stand as the Israelites stood at Mount Sinai, ready
to accept your Torah, my heart ready to take shelter in the
shadow of Your wings and to accept the commandments
which are binding on Your people, the House of Israel.

My God, You have drawn me with cords of love to Your
presence; I have been taught Your commandments and desire
to be part of Your people, the family of Israel. Lead me in the
way of righteousness and humility. Let me not turn my back on
things of old: the family that nurtured me from my childhood,
the friends who have supported and sustained me in my
journey to You, Fountain of Living Waters.

As I enter these waters, let them cover me with Your
graciousness and love and strengthen in me the desire to build
Your kingdom, as it has been said: 'And it shall come to pass in
that day, that living waters shall go out from Jerusalem . . .
And the Eternal One shall be sovereign over all the earth; on
that day You, O Eternal God, shall be One and Your name
one' (Zechariah 14.8–9). May this be Your will. Amen.

To be recited by the rabbi or witness who accompanies the convert to the mikveh:

Blessed are you who come in the name of the Eternal One, we bless you from the house of the Eternal One.

בָּרוּךְ הַבָּא/בְּרוּכָה הַבָּאָה בְּשֵׁם יְיָ.
בֵּרַכְנוּכֶם מִבֵּית יְיָ.

Now let us welcome you as a member of the House of Israel. As our ancestors entered into a covenant of love and faithfulness, so have you entered this day a covenant in which the words of God's Torah will never depart from your lips, as it is written:

I betroth you to me for ever.
I betroth you to me with integrity and justice, with tenderness and love.
I betroth you to me with faithfulness, and you shall know the Eternal One.

וְאֵרַשְׂתִּיךְ לִי לְעוֹלָם
וְאֵרַשְׂתִּיךְ לִי בְּצֶדֶק וּבְמִשְׁפָּט וּבְחֶסֶד
וּבְרַחֲמִים:

וְאֵרַשְׂתִּיךְ לִי בֶּאֱמוּנָה
וְיָדַעַתְּ אֶת-יְהוָֹה:

May the God of Abraham and Sarah, Isaac and Rebecca, Jacob, Leah and Rachel, guide you with love; may the Eternal One inspire you with loyalty and faithfulness; now our people are your people, and our God your God. May God bless you, may the Eternal One open for you an eternal fountain which shall not fail; may God never withhold the waters of life from all those who thirst. Amen.

The Little Boy Who Did Not Know How To Ask

Miri Lawrence

From the questions children ask, and the way they speak, you can tell their character. And according to their character, their parents should teach them. The Torah alludes to four types of child:

One who is wise, one who is wicked, one who is simple and one who does not know how to ask.[1]

I have a son who is unable to ask. He is not a small child, as often depicted in illustrations of the four sons, nor is he a fool or jester, another common feature of Haggadah iconography. He is autistic, which means he has a communication disorder. And in particular, although both his expressive and receptive language develops all the time, he has almost never asked a question.

His diagnosis has changed my life dramatically. It has provided many challenges, introduced me to some wonderful people, heightened my awareness of the achievements of both my son and daughter. But it has also been a very isolating experience. I am very conscious of being 'different', of my family being 'different'.

I suddenly felt that not only had a psychiatrist, in a matter of minutes, taken away the son I knew and loved and given me a new one; I also felt that I was a new person. Frankly, I preferred our former existence. One moment I was a rabbi, happily serving a lovely congregation, and a fulfilled mother with some sort of vision of our future. Suddenly the future seemed a terrifying prospect. Everything I enjoyed became something to feel guilty about. Would my son ever enjoy the things I enjoyed? And this feeling permeated everything, including my religious life. I realized that all the activities I shared with a congregation I might never share with my own son. I could preach to a congregation, I could teach other people's children at various stages of their religious education, but I could not teach my own son. I could not imagine teaching him effectively, as at that point he had almost no language, no comprehension, little eye contact and poor attention span.

Or could I?

The Haggadah continues:

And with the one who does not know how to ask, you must take the first step, as it is written, 'You shall tell your child on that day.'[2]

That duty for a parent to take the initiative and teach the child has unknowingly become a blueprint for many parents of autistic children. With my own son, he did not point to things that were of interest to him, he did not ask questions; very often he did not seem interested in anything at all. I had two choices. I could allow Josh to be a free spirit, not impose my way of living upon him, and hope that he was at least happy. Or, I could try to capture his interest and break through the barriers that seemed against us both. I opted for the second of the two approaches. I felt that it was my responsibility in every way to take the first step, and the second, third and fourth if necessary, if he was not able to take them for himself.

Admittedly, when we first heard that our son was autistic, his Jewish education was the last thing on our minds. I seem to remember our first questions being whether he would go to 'normal' school (a word now dropped from our vocabulary), ever have a friend (some information suggested not), ever have a loving relationship with any one, have a job, live independently?

We had heard of a home-based programme for pre-school children, the Lovaas method, although later, as Joshua also received a place at a nursery two mornings a week for children with communications problems, we adopted a more eclectic approach, combining a number of different methods.

The home programme began with the most simple of tasks, which gradually built up Joshua's understanding and expressive language. First we had to teach him to sit at a table. Tasks were very short, followed by free time. Joshua's confidence was built by giving him achievable tasks, followed by enthusiastic praise and lots of cuddles and tickles and any interaction he enjoyed. At the time, as we struggled to teach him to copy us as we clapped our hands, it seemed that we would never move forward and we would all collapse out of sheer boredom. Yet six months later we struggled to cram in all the tasks Joshua could now complete. By now Joshua was reading, writing, drawing, counting; he understood prepositions, opposites, verbs; he could play a number of games such as pairs and snap and lotto; and he was starting to speak in sentences.

It was during this time, with his new-found confidence and awareness of life around him, that Joshua came home from nursery heartily singing 'Away in a manger' and was soon identifying every piece of Christmas cheer he laid his eyes on. I joked with the head teacher and speech therapist of his school that he was a nice Jewish boy and what were they doing to him, at which she challenged, 'Well, why don't you come and do something for Hanukkah?'

It was at this point that I seriously took stock of his Jewish education. It was a real turning point as I realized that now Joshua had achieved so much, we could and should seriously consider his Jewish upbringing. Teaching a class of autistic individuals was very different from teaching Joshua at home.

Teaching a class was uncharted territory. For while I know my own son pretty well, I did not feel that this qualified me to teach other children with the same condition. This was largely due to the fact that autism is a curious disorder. By definition autistic individuals share certain characteristics, usually defined as difficulties with language and communication, social interaction and imagination. But autism affects individuals in different ways, and I have never met two individuals who are the same. And yet because they share certain basic difficulties and receive the same diagnosis, they are often found with a wide range of abilities in a single class when they attend specialized schools. Having said all this, Hanukkah as a first experience was not too difficult. The visual splendour of the Hanukkah lights, together with *dreidels* (many autistic children love spinning objects) and chocolate Hanukkah *gelt*, made me a popular find and I was invited back for Passover and then asked to the school my son now attends, to an audience of forty children aged between five and eleven years old. Both schools urged me to keep my language to a minimum and to use any visual aids I could find, and I heeded this advice not only in the context of the classroom but also at home.

For it was within the context of home that I was presented with the real challenge. How could I share something that had always been such an integral part of my life with someone I gave life to? Much as I have always cherished the unique bond between Joshua and myself, I had to acknowledge the fact that he did not think like me, or experience the world as I experienced it. And neither of us could successfully communicate to the other in order for me to learn how he felt, how much he understood or what he wanted. Moreover, after five years of training for the rabbinate, I was so aware of the richness of language that is part of our Jewish heritage. How could I reconcile this with the knowledge that my own son could not possibly begin to appreciate Bible stories or the reasons behind our rituals? How could we think of teaching him even the simplest blessing in Hebrew when he did not understand English? All these questions raised themselves to me as we prepared two years ago to celebrate Passover as I had done as a child with family and friends in our home. As I looked at the *Haggadah* and thought about its meaning, 'telling' or 'narration', I despaired at how I could possibly start to tell a child who simply cannot process language.

Having said all this, I did not feel even then as though I were fighting a losing battle. There were some factors that would make life easier for us both. First, there is much that is repetitive in Jewish ritual and liturgy. Things that do not change are often very comforting for the autistic population. The rapidity with which the world around them changes can give rise to problems, feelings of panic and confusion. Many autistic children, Joshua included, will devise elaborate rituals to ensure their own feelings of security. Such rituals and *b'rakhot* that remain unchanged are literally a blessing for families like ours. Our children feel safe and we are not restricted by other unwanted patterns of behaviour, since the rituals are already in place and everyone is happy. So I should not have been stunned when, towards the end of Hanukkah last year, Joshua began to sing the blessings in perfect tune and in crystal-clear Hebrew. It did not matter whether he understood their precise meaning. I'm sure I didn't at five either.

For rituals and sameness are comforting to all of us. They have provided a sense of belonging to the Jewish people when living in strange countries. Some have described autistic individuals as being of a different culture, of being unnerved that the rest of us do things in a different way. Their rituals help them make sense of the world around them when everyone else is speaking a foreign language to them. Many parents have been asked to understand their children in these terms, as being dropped into a different country with a different language, where we do not know which gestures are friendly and which are hostile. As Jews we should not find this too difficult to relate to. And so I began to look more to Jewish rituals. These became more readily accessible than liturgy and interpretation. I think in the past I had thought of prayer largely in terms of language; now ritual was prayer for us, certainly for the immediate future.

In response to this need of autistic children, many programmes contain routine, making clear what will happen each day, and introduce change with great sensitivity. This can be easily applied to Jewish practices in the home, especially Shabbat, which will be remembered from week to week. The rituals remain the same, the blessings are unaltered. Many autistic children, Joshua included, also have good long-term memories and can memorize short prayers and songs. And *Seder* in its meaning of order is ideal for children who need order in their lives.

Secondly, Joshua, like many autistic children, has superb visual skills, and great use of this is made in many teaching methods.

Thus, as Jewish festivals are already rich in visual symbols, as I began to prepare for *Seder* night I aimed to focus on these and make everything I approached as visually appealing as possible. For example, I did not simply recount the story of the Exodus from Egypt, or even use a nicely illustrated book. I found, and in some cases made, bright puppets. One year I enacted the story, using puppets I had made of Moses and Pharaoh. Last year, since Joshua was then able to read, I acted out the story with him, by making a lavish Pharaoh costume which I knew he would want to wear, and even made cardboard pyramids. For the plagues, I was forced to forgo any previous reservations about dwelling on the suffering of the Egyptians. They were just too visually exciting to miss and so I used large puppets of frogs, flies, locusts and sticky spots for boils which amused Joshua and later his classmates.

Since Pesah is such a major festival, a great deal of preparation was undertaken beforehand. I introduced Joshua to all the symbolic foods beforehand so that they would be meaningful to him by *Seder* night. By then he recognised *matzah, haroset* and bitter herbs and could name them. He could also read, and so he had prepared the four questions. But again I approached this in a way that would be most meaningful for Joshua in the light of his difficulties. I knew he would be able to sing *Mah Nishtanah*, much to everyone's delight. He could also probably memorize and read the Hebrew equally well and everyone would be happy. But while he would have had the experience, in effect it would have been entirely meaningless to him. Other parents might be horrified that at a certain age their child was still only able to read the *Mah Nishtanah* in English, but I wanted him to understand the English, as that was a greater challenge than memorizing a chunk of Hebrew. So I rewrote the four questions in a way that had the best chance for comprehension and I taught Joshua the difference between things that are the same and things that are different. Otherwise an expression such as 'Why is this night different from all other nights' would hold absolutely no meaning for him. Equally I worked hard to teach the meaning of each question. For example, I needed to teach him what it meant to lean and what it meant to sit upright. By *Seder* night, when we leant to drink our wine, Joshua was like other children and able to join in whole-heartedly. Equally, even something obviously enjoyable to other children, such as searching for the *afikomen*, had to be taught first. Joshua would be at a total loss roaming around the house with no purpose. By introducing simple games of hiding objects one can build up an understanding of hide and seek to a child who seems to lose interest as soon as an object or person is out of sight.

Once the preparation of the service was under way I was able to undertake some more creative activities with both Joshua and our daughter Natasha, since they were looking forward to the *Seder* itself. We made covers for the specially compiled *Haggadot*, a *Seder* plate and Pesah food. This helped to reinforce the symbols and create a feeling of anticipation that a major celebration was about to take place. Finally, the service itself and narration included much singing and dancing and the use of musical instruments. I was also able to purchase Passover puzzles (a special skill of my son and many others like him), simple books and colouring books. After the event I made a book about our *Seder*, again using simple language and using photographs so that Joshua would have a visual reminder of the day. I now do this for any important family event which helps to reinforce and recall events and can be used again when we begin to prepare for each festival anew. These books can also be taken to school and help Joshua to talk to his class about important events, since he is unlikely, yet, simply to tell his peers much about his experiences at home.

This year, after Natasha had asked to play Moses to

Joshua's Pharaoh, she asked me to tell her more about Moses, as though it were the biggest adventure she had ever heard of. Part of me felt that I had tailored the day to Joshua's needs to such an extent that I had forgotten that she picks up information in an entirely different way and can gain so much from the greater intricacies and subtleties of the story. Yet another part of me felt I had at least succeeded in sustaining her interest sufficiently that she did want to know so much more. So I related the story to her, and answered her questions, and told it again, a little sad that Joshua could not appreciate it in the same way, but filled with hope that each year will be different and that if I need to teach each of my children according to character, I am fulfilling my obligation. The very inclusion of the four sons in the *haggadah* suggests that mine is not the first family to have children with different levels of understanding.

So Judaism has become far more experiential. It is about actions and fulfilling *mitzvot*. The real meaning of prayer and observance has taken on a whole new meaning for my family. The festival of Passover has taught me much that is related to the way I will teach my son in the years to come. I have learnt that whatever the difficulties, I am able to 'tell my son on that day'. I have just had to learn 'how', and my solution has been to do this through my actions: what I can create – artistically, dramatically, musically. In short, I have to explore any method conceivable until I find a way that helps him to understand. And at the same time I have to find an appropriate level for his sister and blend the two together. And I feel I have fulfilled my obligation far more than if I had read the book from cover to cover.

Through this process, and the methods we have used to teach Joshua, I now know that he can be taught, that he can have a Jewish identity, and I do believe that one day he will be able to celebrate fully becoming *Bar Mitzvah*. I never thought two years ago that he would call for me, say he loved me, ask for help, read, write or share his day. But already he has done all those things. In terms of his Jewish education he, too, has achieved what I believed to be impossible. I have found a personal relevance each Passover to the question, 'Why is this night different from all other nights?' The first year it was different because Josh was able to ask the four questions. The second he could help to narrate the Exodus from Egypt. And next year it will be different again. He has shown beyond doubt that he is neither the simple son nor the son who is unable to ask. He is a unique, talented and very special individual. And as such I will continue to teach him according to his character – the more I discover the richness and beauty of it from day to day and year to year.

Appendix

Mah Nishtanah.[3] For Joshua (age four)

> I eat bread.
> Why do I eat *matzah* tonight?
>
> I eat herbs.
> Why do I eat bitter herbs tonight?
>
> I eat herbs.
> Why do I eat herbs with salt water and bitter herbs with *haroset* tonight?
>
> I sit up to eat.
> Why do I lean tonight?

For about a month before Passover a great deal of preparation had been undertaken so that Joshua could identify all of the parts of the four questions. He knew what *matzah* was, had seen *haroset* being made, he had eaten while leaning and had tasted salt water and so on. So by the time *Seder* night came, everything had some meaning to him. He could not assimilate all that new information in one night, and simply hearing the words would not have been enough. He had to see and taste these things on more than one occasion in order to recognize them and be interested and alert to them on *Seder* night.

Play script. For Joshua (age five)

At age four the same script was used with puppets for Moses and Pharaoh as well as the plagues as Josh was not ready to participate until he was five.

Moses: My name is Moses. I am good.
Pharaoh: (played by Josh) My name is Pharaoh. I am bad.
Moses: Can I go home?
Pharaoh: No.
Moses: Then I will give you frogs.
(Moses attacks Pharaoh with large Kermit puppet.)
Pharaoh: Help! Frogs.
Moses: Can I go home?
Pharaoh: No.
Moses: Then I will give you flies.
(Flies on a string buzz round Pharaoh.)
Pharaoh: Help! Flies!
Moses: Can I go home?
Pharaoh: No.
Moses: Then I will give you spots.
(He sticks red office stationery spots on Pharaoh's face.)
Pharaoh: Oh no, spots!
Moses: Can I go home?
Pharaoh: No.
Moses: Then I will give you locusts.
(Moses presents a large glove puppet of a locust making loud chomping noises.)
Pharaoh: Oh no!
Moses: Can I go home?
Pharaoh: No!
Moses: Then I will send lions.
(Moses presents an enormous lion whose mouth can be hand operated.)
Lion: Roar.
Pharaoh: Help!
Lion: Roar.

Pharaoh: HELP!
Lion: ROAR.
Pharaoh: HELP!
Moses: Please can I go home?
Pharaoh: Yes, go home, GO HOME!
Moses: Hurrah!

The play was completed with the singing of *avadim hayinu* – once we are slaves, now we are free – and all the children were given musical instruments to play.

At Joshua's school we omitted the plagues that might frighten the children, such as the plague of darkness, as some of the children become very anxious when the lights are turned down. Likewise it was necessary to keep the story as short as possible, since even with strong visual effects, all ten plagues would be too long for some of them. I also felt that the death of the firstborn, whilst integral to the Exodus from Egypt, might be too traumatic to act out and too difficult to explain and therefore decided to end with a plague of wild beasts. This was in fact enormously successful. Joshua loved screaming for help and the others joined in, and the sight of a gigantic lion seemed to be good enough reason for Pharaoh finally to consent to Moses' departure. The language was deliberately simple and repetitive, with strong visual aids throughout. Likewise the costumes were in sharp contrast. Moses wore a torn sheet, Pharaoh a very shiny appealing costume. He wore a gold hat with purple stripes and jewelled buttons sewn on; a large white shirt with gold yoke; purple ribbon stripes and more jewelled buttons; and a gold sash around his waist. The play opened with Pharaoh carried in on a throne and Moses building pyramids (drawn on cardboard boxes) and simply saying 'Work, work, work' as he presented the pyramids to Pharaoh.

For Joshua aged six

I was able to extend the narration yet further.

Joshua's reading and comprehension had again moved

forward and I was able to make the language a little less simplistic. The plagues were also presented in full.

Soft white balls that didn't hurt when hurled were thrown at Pharaoh for the plague of hail with Pharaoh exclaiming, 'Ow, that hurts.' Blackcurrant juice made a good glass of water from the river that had turned to blood. The lights went off for the plague of darkness as neither Josh or Natasha were afraid of temporary darkness. I still felt it was inappropriate to enact the final plague, but felt it must be acknowledged. I therefore introduced the Exodus with a short narration, and then returned to the narration for the final plague and subsequent Exodus from Egypt. For the parting of the waters, I used an ocean drum and this was followed by music from the *Prince of Egypt*. Joshua has always been a huge fan of animated films and loved the soundtrack from the *Prince of Egypt*, which we played many times during the lead up to Pesah. The ocean drum and music created a fantastic atmosphere. We had deliberately used humour for the plagues, as humour has always been a key to involving Joshua in activities. The drum and music brought a seriousness to the room and a chance for people to take a few moments for quiet personal reflection.

How to Pray When You Can't Pray

Margaret Jacobi and Sheila Shulman

There are times for all of us when it is difficult to pray. There may be different reasons. We may have experienced a tragedy in our life, illness or bereavement. This may make us question the words of prayers or the very idea of praying. Or our emotions might overpower us as we try to pray. We may be going through a period of spiritual drought, when the effort of prayer does not seem to have any meaning. We may simply not see the point of praying any more.

If we are unable to pray, the question that follows is, 'Why should we?' Why should we bother to make the effort when it seems difficult or pointless? Again, there are a number of possible answers, and they will not all be given here. We would simply suggest that we are trying to answer the question because for some women finding a way to pray when they cannot is important. It is not a question of 'should'. Prayer is not something that can be compelled. Rather, finding a way to pray can meet a need and be part of the process of finding healing.

For some women, who pray regularly and for whom prayer forms an important part of their daily routine, the very disruption of this routine may be a loss. They may want to carry on praying, but suddenly find that the words of their prayers stick in their mouth and they are unable to continue. For others who have not prayed regularly before, paradoxically, prayer may provide a help and support, even though God[1] at first seems distant and alien. Although at first difficult, prayer may provide a focus for understanding one's feelings, and in that sense may be 'therapeutic'. It may also lead to a deeper experience, which may be felt as a sense of contact with the Divine.

In such circumstances, turning to the traditional prayers can be an important start, even though, to those unfamiliar with them, they might seem to come from a distant world. They provide words when one cannot find one's own, and even if we disagree with them, they provide a starting point for a conversation – with tradition, with God or with ourselves – in which we may find meaning. We may also find startling echoes of our own feelings in the traditional prayers. The Psalms in particular, which have provided help and comfort for generations of Jews, often express a sense of longing, of abandonment and even of despair. But turning to the words of tradition may require some preparation. It may not be possible to turn to the words of the Psalms and immediately find a resonance with them. There may be other stages to go through, and other means of finding a way to pray. On the other hand, one may be startled by a resonance which is totally unexpected. There may be words which have been passed over before, but which suddenly have a meaning because they are read again when circumstances are different. Or they may be words which are new to one and which startle in the way they seem to say what one has been needing to hear.

Since bereavement of one sort or another (widely defined – a bereavement may, for example, be the end of a relationship or the loss of a job) is often a reason why a woman cannot pray, it may be helpful to think about some of the stages of bereavement as defined by Elisabeth Kübler-Ross,[2] and their relationship to possible approaches to prayer. As Kübler-Ross herself says, the stages are not necessarily linear. A person may go from a later stage back to an earlier one and may not go through all the stages. Rather, they are a guide to the sort of reactions that might occur after bereavement. In a similar way, we will use some of the stages of bereavement as indications of the ways we might feel when we are finding it difficult to pray, and consider approaches to prayer that might be appropriate.

The first stage of bereavement is a feeling of shock and numbness. The full implications of the bad news are not fully taken in and their implications have not been realized. Emotions are not yet surfacing. This shock of numbness is eloquently expressed by two words in the Torah. After Aaron's two sons have mysteriously and suddenly died, it is stated: '*Vayidom Aharon* – and Aaron was silent' (Leviticus 10.3). It is also the stage of bereavement to which the saying of R. Simeon ben Elazar in the Mishnah may well be applied: 'Do not comfort people in the hour when their dead lie before them' (Avot 4.23). Words are not a help at this time. Silence is the only appropriate response. So there may be a time when it is not even appropriate to try to pray. Again, the Mishnah appears to recognize this when it exempts someone suffering from acute loss from saying the *Sh'ma* (Berachot 3.1). This may be seen as a preparation for prayer, so that if words of prayer come to mind they may be said. Or it may be a time to start to allow oneself to feel. It is an individual matter how long to stay in silence. It may be difficult to spend long, as emotions are ready to burst out but are still too painful to release. Every person will find what is possible and helpful for themselves. But silence may be necessary before it is possible to start to pray.

After the numbness, anger follows. This can be a particularly difficult stage for women, who are socialized not to feel anger. But it is important to recognize that anger is legitimate. Not only is the feeling real and justifiable. As well, Judaism accepts that it is possible to feel anger towards God without abandoning God or Jewish tradition. Again, the Psalms may be helpful, because they sometimes recall a struggle to find God again after feeling abandoned. For example, in Psalm 77 we read: 'I cried out to God, I shouted out, I cried aloud to God, who heard me. In the day of my distress I searched for the Eternal One, my hand was stretched out all night long, my soul refused all comfort. I moaned when I remembered God; as I lay thinking, my spirit sank' (Psalm 77.1–3). Psalm 30 says: 'Eternal One, Your favour set me on a mountain stronghold – but then

You hid Your face, and I was in terror. To You, Eternal One, I call, from the Eternal One I ask pity' (Psalm 30.7–8). But at the same time, the Psalms may themselves provoke feelings of anger if we do not feel the same sense of trust and support that the Psalmist felt. Very often, the Psalms have been written from a place of safety. They do recall a time of turmoil and distress, but they are written from the point of view of someone who has come through that period and found a new sense of security and assurance. When one is in the middle of a time of turmoil, one may need to find expression for that and one may not be ready to recite the words of affirmation found in the Psalms.

The words of the traditional prayers, too, may make us angry when they seem to say things we cannot believe. There have been times, when I have visited someone who is seriously ill, when to say of God the words *rofei holim* – who heals the sick – has been impossible because they seemed so far from the truth I had experienced.

There are words from our tradition, older and more recent, which may express for us the anger we feel. An eloquent expression of anger is found in the way that the chasidic leader Levi Yitzchak of Berditchev argues against God to persuade him to show mercy to humankind. Similarly, an eighteenth-century *tehine* written by Sarah Rebecca Rachel Leah, daughter of Rabbi Yokel Segal Horowitz, puts words of anger and rebellion into the mouth of Rachel: 'Rachel went up before God with a bitter cry, and spoke: "Eternal God, Your mercy is certainly greater than the mercy of any human being. Moreover, I had compassion on my sister Leah . . . No matter that it caused me great pain; because of my great compassion for my sister, I told her the signs. Thus, even more so, it is undoubtedly fitting for you, God, who are compassionate and gracious, to have mercy." '³

More overt and raw anger is expressed in a poem called 'Healing after a Miscarriage' by Merl Feld, which must express feelings other women have shared in similar circumstances:

Nothing helps. I taste ashes
in my mouth. My eyes are flat,
dead. I want no platitudes,
no stupid shallow comfort.
I hate all pregnant women,
all new mothers, all soft babies . . .[4]

Reading such words may help us to find our own words and to
give expression to our anger. At this stage, it may actually help
to have a male image of God, a figure at whom anger can be
directed. To express anger will in itself be a form of prayer: it is
a way of acknowledging God, making a connection and forming a relationship. Beyond the difficulty women often feel at
expressing anger at all, it may feel wrong to address God in
overtly angry terms. But knowing it has been done before can
help us to express the anger within us. It may help, too, to
know that being angry with God does not diminish the Divine.
When we express our anger, we may be able to move beyond it
and come nearer to God in prayer.

    After anger, Kübler-Ross describes a stage of bargaining.
This may be seen as a time to question and discuss, in an
attempt to come to terms with our situation. It is a time when
one can read the prayers and argue with them. One can disagree with the words and yet try to find meaning in them. It
may involve intellectualizing, thinking about the words rather
than reacting to them on an emotional level. This can lead to
different ways of understanding the words of prayer. For
example, *rofei holim* has been reinterpreted in various ways. It
may be understood as meaning that God helps human beings
to bring about healing, and that we are acting as partners with
God in the healing process. Alternatively, one may think of
God as healing souls, helping people to find an inner peace
even in the face of physical suffering. Not everyone will find
such reinterpretations satisfactory, but by thinking about the
words of prayers in different ways, a woman may start to find
answers to her questioning.

    The questioning may involve further exploration, reading

books of theology which consider the problem of suffering. Reading about how others have come to terms with pain and suffering can help one to come to terms with one's own grief. Again, every woman will have different needs and find different ways to fulfil them. But at this stage, Jewish study may be both an end to itself and a way to prayer.[5]

If by questioning one can reach some sort of understanding, it may then be possible to start to pray again in the sense of returning to the words of tradition and saying them with a growing sense of *kavannah* – of intention and focus. This will not be a smooth process. Questioning may lead to further anger, or to denial and a questioning of the worth of the whole enterprise of prayer. But perhaps prayer will no longer feel impossible, but will begin to feel worthwhile and meaningful, at least at times.

Finally, there comes a time of acceptance. There is a realization that this is how things are and an ability to face them with a certain degree of equanimity. As Kübler-Ross says: 'Acceptance should not be mistaken for a happy stage, it is almost void of feeling.'[6] It is a time when one may need to be alone and regain one's strength in solitude. There will also still be times of anger, frustration, bewilderment and doubt. But there will also be times of hope. Prayer may have meaning again, and through it one may find oneself closer to God than before. The relationship may be strengthened by the struggle that has been, by the honest anger that has been expressed and by the separation that has been experienced as loss. Out of the darkness of distance, one may be able to find the faith expressed in a poem by the early twentieth-century English poet Nina Davis Salaman:

Of Prayer . . .

   'Out of the depths I call Thee' – What were life
   Lacking such solace to its lonely pain?
   How could the dumb heart suffer, and sustain
   The sorrow and the bitterness and strife;

And know the gloom and dream not of the light?
They watching for the morning wait not so,
Not as the soul waits, yearning from its woe
Upward to some unknown unending height.

And though no sign nor help come, and no voice,
nor any knowledge from the silent peak,
Trustfully from its pain the soul shall speak,
'Out of the depths I call Thee', and rejoice.[7]

Fertility

Menarche Ritual

Lee Wax

One of the most significant experiences in a woman's life is when she starts her periods. No matter at what age it happens, the physical transition from child to woman is sudden, dramatic and irrevocable. It is intensely important, both physically and emotionally, in that the young woman now has the potential within her to have children of her own. And it is also of spiritual importance to acknowledge the blessing of reaching this new stage in her life. Yet in Judaism there has been no formal recognition of this experience, and this is a lost opportunity. As Jewish women, we should be creating and conducting ceremonies to mark ritually the time when our periods start.

I am aware that some young women feel embarrassed about starting to menstruate, and some would feel that a public ceremony is the last thing they would want! I certainly would not advocate imposing a ritual on anyone if she didn't want it. However, I do think that we have a role to play in changing perceptions about our bodily functions, particularly menstruation. It is a ceremony which should mark the transition from child to woman, and which should recognize the holiness in that transition. It should be a welcome into womanhood, by other women, giving emotional and practical support, but above all, it should be a celebration of the new physical state: the potential – the holy potential – to give life.

The ceremony which for me best fits the occasion is an adaptation of the *Havdalah* ceremony. *Havdalah* means 'separation', and when we perform the ritual on *Motza'ey Shabbat* we mark the transition between the Sabbath and the working week. We have wine, a plaited candle and sweet-smelling

spices to represent different aspects of Shabbat, and to use our
senses in our farewell to Shabbat and our welcoming in the
new week. It is a beautiful ceremony, and it is sweetly wistful
both in its melodies and words of longing. I think a separation
ceremony works very well as the basis for a menarche ritual,
for three main reasons.

First, because of the separation between childhood and
womanhood. Secondly, the potent symbols of the ceremony –
the wine, the spices, the fire – fit the celebration of physical
changes as well as having strong metaphorical associations.
Lastly, there is something about the wistfulness of the
Havdalah ceremony, its wanting to prolong the Shabbat, not
wanting quite to let go, which is terribly important, because it
helps us hold on to the sadness at letting go, in our case, of
childhood. As you will see below, I have changed the order of
the three blessings, so that the young woman's blessing is the
last.

The menarche is a basic ritual, which can be used as it is, or
adapted to be more personal. The ritual is essentially for the
young woman and her mother, together with other female
relatives and friends – although some young women might feel
comfortable with male relatives there too.

Above all, any ritual should be a way of recognizing a young
woman's transition as God-given, as sacred, of positively
marking the experience of having periods, and of offering the
young woman solidarity and support.

The ritual (directions are in italics).

*Sit in a circle, with the Havdalah set in the centre. Fill the cup
with wine, open the spice box, and light the candle. If you can,
sing something together. It could be anything you like, a niggun
– and* Hinei mah tov u'manaim stevet ahim gam yahad *('Behold
how good and pleasant it is for brothers to sit together') always
works well (because people either know it or pick it up
quickly!). If you use the words with* Hinei mah tov, *you may like
to substitute the word* 'ahayot' *(sisters) for* 'ahim' *(brothers).*

The wine

Mother speaks about her daughter, then picks up the cup of wine, and ends with this prayer:

Eloheinu velohei avoteinu v'immoteinu, our God and God of our ancestors, I ask Your blessing on my daughter ...... as she enters this new phase in her life. I have been blessed with watching her grow from a child into a woman, and I have grown with her. I have been privileged to care for her in her dependence, and nurture her towards independence. May You grant me wisdom in supporting her through her teenage and adult years. The wine I hold in my hand is a symbol of God's fruitfulness and God's provision – reflected in our ability to bear children and care for them. It also celebrates the sweetness of this moment. May my daughter's life contain sweetness and fruitfulness.

בָּרוּךְ אַתָּה יְיָ אֱלֹהֵינוּ מֶלֶךְ הָעוֹלָם בּוֹרֵא פְּרִי הַגָּפֶן.

Barukh attah Adonai, eloheinu melekh ha-olam, borei p'ri ha-gafen.

Blessed are You, Eternal One, sovereign of the universe, who creates the fruit of the vine.

Mother has a sip, passes the cup to her daughter, then all present drink a sip of the wine.

The candle

Someone else who is close (a grandmother, an aunt, a cousin or a friend) speaks about the young woman, and then picks up the plaited candle. She says the following prayer:

This plaited candle reflects an interweaving. As women we know the experience of having to hold together several strands in our lives, and we know the beauty and richness that this can give us. We see the individual strands coming together into one strong flame, symbolic of the strength and inspiration that can come when women celebrate together. The flame itself represents God's fire, the fire of creation, the fire of inspiration, and the light of the *Sh'khinah*, God's presence here on earth. May

...... experience these in her life ahead as a Jewish woman. And
may the *Sh'khinah* always guide her and shield her.

*All present hold up their hands towards the light, to see the
flame reflected in their fingernails. Say together:*

בָּרוּךְ אַתָּה יְיָ אֱלֹהֵינוּ מֶלֶךְ הָעוֹלָם בּוֹרֵא מְאוֹרֵי הָאֵשׁ.
*Barukh attah Adonai, eloheinu melekh ha-olam, borei m'orei
ha-eish.*
Blessed are You, Eternal One, sovereign of the universe, who
creates the lights of the fire.

The spices

*The young woman herself now has an opportunity to speak,
and then picks up the spice box and says:*

Eloheinu velohei avoteinu v'immoteinu, God and God of
our ancestors, I give thanks for reaching this time. I am grateful for the love and support of the women here today, and pray
that I will continue to feel supported and guided by them in the
months and years ahead. As I become a Jewish woman, may I
learn from the strength and wisdom of other Jewish women,
past and present. At this very important stage in my life, I
invoke the strength and teachings of the four matriarchs to
help me on my way.

Elohei Sarah, God of Sarah, give me strength and courage as
I leave the familiarity of childhood, and go forward on my
journey into an unknown stage in my life.

Elohei Rivkah, God of Rebecca, may I learn to bear the
physical discomfort of menstruation, and know that as a blessing, as a sign of the miraculous, God-given potential to create
life within me.

Elohei Rachel, God of Rachel, may I always treat my body
with pride and with respect.

vElohei Leah, and God of Leah, with Your blessing may I
one day come to know the joy of motherhood.

She picks up the spice box, and continues to read.

'On Shabbat, these sweet-smelling spices represent the *n'shamah yeterah*, the additional soul which we receive on Shabbat, and we smell them to breathe in the last essences of the day of rest, to take it with us into the working week. Today, though, the sweet smell represents something different – the spirit of childhood. I am excited about entering a new stage in my life, and I hope that I will always be guided by Torah and my tradition as I move into womanhood. But may I also take with me a *n'shamah yeterah*, the aspects of childhood which I should not want to lose in adulthood – honesty, creativity, spontaneity, fun and energy – and the love of learning.

I am grateful for the love and support of all of those who have brought me to this time, and hope I will be able to look to you for your wisdom and guidance in the months and years ahead.

בָּרוּךְ אַתָּה יְיָ אֱלֹהֵינוּ מֶלֶךְ הָעוֹלָם בּוֹרֵא מִינֵי בְשָׂמִים

Barukh attah Adonai, eloheinu melekh ha-olam, borei minei v'samim

Blessed are You, Eternal One, sovereign of the universe, who creates all kinds of spices.

She smells the sweet spices first, then each person there does the same. All present say or sing the she-heheyanu:

בָּרוּךְ אַתָּה יְיָ אֱלֹהֵינוּ מֶלֶךְ הָעוֹלָם שֶׁהֶחֱיָנוּ וְקִיְּמָנוּ וְהִגִּיעָנוּ לַזְּמַן הַזֶּה.

Barukh attah Adonai, eloheinu melekh ha-olam, she-heheyanu, v'kiyy'manu v'higgi'anu la-z'man ha-zeh

Blessed are You Eternal One, sovereign of the universe, who has kept us alive, and sustained us, and brought us to this time.

The ritual finishes with this blessing:

בָּרוּךְ אַתָּה יְיָ אֱלֹהֵינוּ מֶלֶךְ הָעוֹלָם שֶׁעָשַׂנִי אִשָּׁה.

Barukh attah Adonai, eloheinu melekh ha-olam, she-asani ishah

Blessed are You Eternal One, sovereign of the universe, who has made me a woman.

Simhat Brit M'ugelet:
Rejoicing in Becoming Round.
A Pregnancy Ritual

Marcia Plumb

Simhat Brit M'ugelet means a Celebration of the Covenant that Comes From Becoming Round *(m'ugelet)*. The circle is a powerful mystical shape in Judaism. The Zohar, a thirteenth-century Jewish mystical book, says that a circle appeared at the first moment of creation, a *'qutra' degulma' na'if be'azaqa'*, 'misty matter set in a circle'. A poem found in *Motherprayer* celebrates this idea beautifully.

> At the primal moment,
> suddenly,
> *qutra' degulma' na'if be'azaqa,*
> misty matter set in a circle.
> At our first moment,
> we are set in a circle,
> mists swirling, connecting,
> then dividing,
> segmenting,
> travelling,
> coming to the womb,
> Enclosed in the primal circle,
> exploding within.
> Into my womb comes the embryo:
> circles within circles,
> embryos within womb
> wombs within women

women within worlds
worlds within galaxies
circles within circles
wheels within wheels
mists of matter,
set in a circle
qutra' degulma' na'if be'azaqa.[1]

The *Simhat Brit M'ugelet* was a ceremony to mark and celebrate the new circularity of my body; in other words, my pregnancy, and how far I'd come in appreciating it. As it says in *Motherprayer*, 'There are three elements in the affirmation of pregnancy: acceptance of responsibility for the baby to come, invocation of God's participation, and the initiation of a woman into a new state of existence.'[2]

I was aware that for me becoming pregnant and thus eventually a mother was somewhat frightening. Since first discovering I was pregnant, I had moved a long way in appreciating this experience. When the ceremony took place, I was five months pregnant. I loved the baby inside me, and the new adventure I, and my husband Michael, were on together. Thus, I wanted a *'simhah'* ritual, a celebration ritual to mark this time, and moment, in my life.

Because I was still apprehensive, however, I wanted this ceremony to help move me closer towards the realization that I was in fact a mother already, even though the baby had not yet been born. Caring for the baby inside me was a type of covenantal relationship. I had certain obligations towards the unborn child, such as eating healthily, resting, staying stress-free, and I wanted this ceremony to help me in my attempts to fulfil them. I also needed the support, guidance and experience of women who had either had children before or had major life changes, regardless of whether those changes had involved children. I knew that I would need their support throughout the pregnancy and beyond.

Via the ceremony, I hoped to gain encouragement from my friends and family as my body became bigger and rounder, and to hold on to that encouragement during the moments I felt elephantine instead of beautiful and 'womanly'!

Finally, I hoped to receive the blessings of my friends as I travelled on this new journey. I knew their blessings would spiritually help to carry me as I went on my way.

Needs

Participants: I invited only women, plus my father, who with my mother was visiting from the States. I decided that, although a man, he had 'earned' the right to come, and I wanted his blessing. Each person was asked to bring a thought or words of advice on having children, or making life changes, and a blessing or hope for me.

A circle of chairs: We sat in a circle to reinforce the theme of 'roundness'.

Glass beads: My parents and I chose these beads from a bead shop with love and fun, to be strung on a piece of leather during the ritual. They will serve as a reminder of the love and support of the participants and will possibly be taken into labour, and later hung on the baby's wall. All who later visit will be invited to add a bead to that string or a new string.

Bowl of water in the centre of the circle: The water acts as a symbol of birth waters, and the waters of the Red Sea, and Miriam dancing the women through those miraculous waters. The bowl of water is also a symbol of washing the feet, a biblical welcoming ceremony. This water was used to wash my hands, rather than feet, as a welcoming gesture into motherhood and this new stage of my life.

A tallit: I had bought this particular *tallit* in the early days of my pregnancy, as my 'pregnancy *tallit*'. It is special in that it has the names of the matriarchs on the four corners. I feel when wearing it that all the Jewish women throughout the centuries, including the matriarchs, surround me with their strength, fears, survival techniques, and support. We will wrap the baby in this *tallit* at the naming.

The Ceremony

Introductions

Matrilineage – I invited each woman to introduce herself with her name, and then to name the women ancestors in her family, as well as women who had been guides to her in her own life. As an example, I introduced myself as Marcia Ruth, bat (daughter of) Lois, bat Sadie and Libby (my grand-mothers), bat Ruth (my mother-in-law), bat Jane (a friend by whom I was inspired).

Another example of a matrilineage, written by Tikva Freymer-Kinsky, is:

'I am Tikva, scholar, writer, teacher,
mother of Meira and Eitan,
daughter of Elyse, ballet dancer, clothes designer,
refugee from Paris,
mother of two.
Elyse is daughter of Helene,
grande dame of Latvia,
widowed young,
refugee to Paris,
mother of four.
Helen, daughter of Sarah (?)
mother of fourteen.'[3]

Blessing

We then recited two blessings and a prayer:

בָּרוּךְ אַתָּה יְיָ אֱלֹהֵינוּ מֶלֶךְ הָעוֹלָם שֶׁהֶחֱיָנוּ וְקִיְּמָנוּ וְהִגִּיעָנוּ לַזְּמַן הַזֶּה.
Barukh altah Adonai, eloheinu melech ha-olam, she heheyanu,
vikiyy'manu, v'higgiyanu laz'man ha-zeh
Blessed are you O God, who has sustained us, kept us alive and brought us to this moment in our lives.

Blessed are You, *Sh'khinah*, who in wisdom formed women's bodies and created in us unique openings, passageways, organs and glands. These are known and revealed to You. If one of these opens when it should close or closes when it should open, it would be impossible for us to live and sustain ourselves or to create and sustain our children.

Blessed are you Sh'khinah, healer of flesh, who creates and sustains our bodies in wondrous ways.[4]

בְּרוּכָה אַתְּ שְׁכִינָה מְקוֹר הַחַיִּים שֶׁעֲשִׂתַנִי אִשָּׁה.

B'rukhah at Sh'khinah, m'kor hayyim, she-astani Isha.

Blessed are you, *Sh'khinah*, source of life, who has made me a woman.[5]

Covenant

I then made a promise to my unborn child with the following adaptation of a reading: 'Knowing that it is not easy to be partner with God, knowing it is hard to be member to a covenant, I state my desire to observe all the obligations of this covenant. As the mother of Samson before his birth, I too will refrain from drinking wine, beer or other alcohol, and from eating impure foods. I will not smoke, use drugs, or drink coffee or (only occasionally!) caffeine. I will care for my body and the life I shelter within me. I will be as stress-free as possible. I will do all the exercises I can to prepare my body and my soul, and to help this child into the world. I declare that I will prepare to give my child a faithful home in Israel, and I will learn even as it grows within me, the depths of mother-love.'

Participants' blessings and words of wisdom

I then asked each participant to offer their thoughts and to pick a bead and string it.

Washing of hands

I asked all to gather around the water and wash everyone's hands that needed courage for a particular life change, and then to wash mine. It was great fun and felt lovely.

We then ended with champagne!

For further consideration

I was inspired in the preparation of this ritual by the following poems from *Motherprayer:*

> In good mystic's fashion I will contemplate my navel.
> My navel has grown large
> and open and deep.
> It leads me inward.
> My stomach grows large and round,
> like a circle drawn for meditation,
> my own mandala.
>
> I will contemplate my navel,
> meditate on my mandala.
> My flesh grows transparent, and I can see inside.
> Inside I see a tree, growing inward
> flowering in another navel
> 'umbilicus' of my child.
> The tree pulses with life and blood
> bringing nourishment to the life within.
>
> At the end of the tree, the amnion,
> beautiful ball, corona of loveliness.
> Little spaceship that holds the growing being.
> Little voyager from eternity,
> from the single cell,
> ground of all being.
>
> Star voyager of the inner heavens,
> visitor from the beginning of time,
> time-traveller from past to future,

child of the eons of humankind,
child to me.[6]

Covenant prayer

For Eve first recognized this bond of creation, affirming it at
the birth of her first son,
when she stated: I have created a man with the Lord.
God who creates us has created in woman
the power to continue and participate in God's creations on
earth.
I come today to affirm this partnership with God:
In my womb You form the child,
in my womb I nourish it.
There You form and number the limbs,
there I contain and protect them.
You who can see the child in my depths,
I who can feel the kicks and the turns,
together we count the months,
together we plan the future.
Flesh of my flesh, form of Your form,
another human upon the earth, a home for God in this, our
world.[7]

At the Moment of Birth

Sybil Sheridan

בָּרוּךְ הַבָּא/בְּרוּכָה הַבָּאָה בְּשֵׁם יְיָ.
Barukh/a habah/haba'ah b'sheim Adonai,
Blessed be s/he who comes in the name of the Eternal.

My child, I have known you for many months.
I have felt the first stirrings of your limbs firm and harden against my belly.
I have seen your faint form on the hospital scanner.
But only now do I see you in your wondrous wholeness, your wondrous smallness, your wondrous perfection.
I hear your cry, I feel your smoothness, I smell your newness and I give thanks.

Eternal, our God, how magnificent is your name throughout the earth.
Your splendour is recounted over the heavens.
From the mouths of babies and sucklings you have founded strength. . .
When I see your heavens and the work of your fingers,
the moon and stars that you established,
what is humanity that you remember it?
and the children of human beings that you take notice?
and that you have made them little less than angels?
and have crowned them with glory and honour?[1]

And God created humanity in the divine image. In the image of God was humanity created. Male and female God created them.[2]
Thus says the Eternal, your redeemer, who formed you from the womb, I the Eternal make all things;[3]

There are three *partners* in the making of a person: the blessed Holy One, the father and the mother. The father and the mother create the bodily form ...... the blessed Holy One gives the child spirit and soul, beauty of appearance, the powers of speech, sight and hearing, the ability to walk, understanding and intelligence.[4]

The pain of labour is over, the apprehension and fear is past. I have experienced a miracle in the creating of you.

בָּרוּךְ אַתָּה יְיָ אֱלֹהֵינוּ מֶלֶךְ הָעוֹלָם הַגּוֹמֵל לְחַיָבִים טוֹבוֹת שֶׁגְּמָלַנִי כָּל-טוֹב

Barukh attah Adonai Eloheinu melekh ha-olam, ha-gomel l'hayyavim tovot she-g'malani kol tov.

We praise you, Eternal, our God, ruler of the universe, who shows goodness to the undeserving, that you have shown every goodness to me.

Those attending the birth respond

מִי שֶׁגְּמָלַךְ כָּל-טוֹב הוּא יִגְמָלֵךְ כָּל-טוֹב

Mi she-g'malakh kol tov hu yigm'leikh kol tov.

May God who has shown goodness to you, continue to favour you with all that is good.

Simhat Bat:
Welcoming a Daughter

Sylvia Rothschild

A ritual to take place on the eighth day.

You will need: A taper and a seven-branched candlestick.

A soft cushion or pillow, and a large soft cloth with which to cover it.

An empty chair.

Choose two adults to act as supporters for the child. As a taper is lit, they bring the child into the room on a cushion covered with a soft cloth. The cloth may be embroidered with the child's names in English and Hebrew, with the date of birth, with images of pomegranate and etrog and of the Tree of Life, with a seven-branched candlestick. It may be embroidered later, to be used to wrap a *sefer torah*, or else made into a bag to wrap and protect the shabbat candlesticks and *kiddush* cup to be given to the child.

Those present waiting to welcome the child sing a song of welcome. It might be the child's own name sung to a soothing tune.

Or a fragment of Psalm 24:

'The earth and its fullness belong to the Eternal, the world and those who dwell in it;

for it is God who set it on the seas and made it firm upon the depths.

Who may ascend the mountain of the Eternal?

And who may stand in the place of God's holiness?

The one whose hands are clean, whose heart is pure . . .'

Or the first verse of Psalm 113:

'Hallelujah!
Servants of the Eternal, praise the name of the Eternal.
May the name of the Eternal be blessed now and evermore.'

Or the song *Y'did Nefesh*:

'Beloved of the soul, merciful father,
draw your servant to your own desires . . .'

As the child is brought in to the welcoming sound, she is
taken to the special empty chair, and placed in the arms of an
older woman relative or special figure in her life, who then sits
in the chair.

Her supporters say:

מַה-נּוֹרָא הַמָּקוֹם הַזֶּה אֵין זֶה כִּי אִם-בֵּית אֱלֹהִים וְזֶה שַׁעַר הַשָּׁמָיִם.

*Mah norah ha-makkom ha-zeh, ein zeh ki im beit elohim,
ve-zeh sha'ar ha-shamayim*
How awesome is this place, this is none other than the house of
God, and this is the gate of heaven (Genesis 18.17).

All present say: בְּרוּכָה הַבָּאָה בְּשֵׁם יְיָ.
B'rukhah ha-ba'ah b'sheim adonai.
Blessed is she who comes in God's name.

The leader says: We welcome into our community ...... As
the sign of her entry into the yoke of the
mitzvot, we light this *menorah*, sign of our
people from earliest times, and with each of
the seven candles we remember the seven
prophetesses who came before her and who
added their distinctive specialness to our
community.[1]
Light the first candle in honour of Sarah,
princess and matriarch.
'May you be like Sarah, strong and wise,
whose voice was listened to.'

Light the second candle in honour of Miriam, prophetess and leader.

> 'May you be like Miriam, who sang and danced in joy with her sisters at the Reed Sea.'

Light the third candle in honour of Deborah.

> 'May you be like Deborah, who judged wisely, a woman of fire.'

Light the fourth candle in honour of Hannah.

> 'May you be like Hannah, who prayed and who exulted in God.'

Light the fifth candle in honour of Abigail.

> 'May you be like Abigail, hospitable and independently minded.'

Light the sixth candle in honour of Hulda.

> 'May you be like Hulda the prophetess, who lived in Jerusalem and who spoke God's word.'

Light the seventh candle in honour of Esther.

> 'May you be like Esther, brave and clever, who saved her people through her own relationships.'

The supporters say:

> We light these lights to proclaim the work of our mothers, and to ask for blessing so that ...... may follow their example. We name her today, we bring her into the company of our people, we accept the *mitzvot* on her behalf, and we pray that she too will hear the voice of God, and that her voice will be heard in our world. She stood with us at Sinai, we stand here with her today. As she is made in the image of God, we call down God's presence to dwell with her throughout her life.

A *mi she-berakh* can be said here over a glass of *kiddush* wine, written by the family stating the special hopes for their daughter.

Beginning:

מִי שֶׁבֵּרַךְ אֲבוֹתֵינוּ וְאִמּוֹתֵינוּ אַבְרָהָם וְשָׂרָה יִצְחָק וְרִבְקָה יַעֲקֹב וְרָחֵל וְלֵאָה, הוּא יְבָרֵךְ אֶת-הַיַּלְדָּה הַזֹּאת ......

Mi she-berakh avoteinu Avraham v'Sarah, Yitzhak v'Rivkah, Ya'akov v'Rachel v'Leah, hu y'varekh et ha-yaldah ha-zot ......

May the One who blessed our ancestors Abraham and Sarah, Isaac and Rebecca. Jacob and Rachel and Leah, bless this girl ......

Ending:

...... Her responsibilities are many, she will work in the world, yet she will not lose the privilege of welcoming in the Shabbat, and so we give her now her own Shabbat candlesticks and kiddush cup. May she use them in the future to create her own Jewish home, and to welcome in her children to *k'hillat Yisrael*, the community of Israel. They are a sign of her entry into the Covenant today, that she may use them to demonstrate that Covenant every seventh day, and take her place within it.

All say:

בָּרוּךְ אַתָּה יְיָ אֱלֹהֵינוּ מֶלֶךְ הָעוֹלָם בּוֹרֵא פְּרִי הַגָּפֶן.

Barukh attah Adonai, eloheinu melekh ha-olam, borei p'ri ha-gafen.

Blessed are You God, Sovereign of the universe, Creator of the fruit of the vine.

בָּרוּךְ אַתָּה יְיָ אֱלֹהֵינוּ מֶלֶךְ הָעוֹלָם שֶׁהֶחֱיָנוּ וְקִיְּמָנוּ וְהִגִּיעָנוּ לַזְּמַן הַזֶּה.

Barukh attah Adonai, eloheinu melekh ha-olam, she-heheyanu, v'kiy'manu, v'higi'anu laz'man ha-zeh.

Blessed are You God, Sovereign of the universe, who has kept us alive, and sustained us, and brought us to this time.

AMEN.

Infertility

Responding to the Cry –
Reactions to Childlessness

Jacqueline Tabick

The letters held in my hand spoke of so much unresolved pain. Stillbirths. Miscarriages. The end of the line medically. No hope of another child. And no public mourning rituals to support the couple. Or another case. A visit to a maternity ward, but no rejoicing in sight. The baby had died at eight months gestation because the mother had caught a nasty flu virus. The mother had recently converted to Judaism. In her former faith, the priest would have come and baptized the baby and given her the comfort of an old and established ritual. From us, words of sympathy, even a private burial service, but it was just not enough.

In past generations, such sad events were an accepted part of life. In fact, infant mortality before the age of thirty days was so high it was regarded as a kindness that no *shivah* or other mourning rites were commanded.

In contrast, today, the relationship between parent and child begins in the first weeks of pregnancy when the mother lies on the examination table and the miracle of conception unfolds before her eyes on the screen of the scanner. Already, the heart can be seen beating, the backbone is visible, and the buds that will develop into what one hopes will be strong, healthy limbs are already present. And so few babies die, it feels so un-natural, so wrong, so unfair, when it happens to you.

And so, thanks to the efforts of some very special people, the idea of a specific Remembrance Service for the 'might have beens', the 'vanished dreams', the 'defunct hopes', was explored and brought to fruition.

And the stories that emerged! The grandmother who came

to mourn the loss of a grandchild that very week. A cot death at six months, but the father was not Jewish and no religious rituals had occurred, so the service gave the grandmother space to mourn among her people.

And the deaths that were still so present although they had happened decades before. The stillborn son, whose burial was organized by the Orthodox grandfather and the mother was never allowed to mourn, or visit the grave, because she was never informed where he lay. The unmarried teenage mother, forced to have an abortion, who now came supported by her daughter and granddaughter, finally allowed to acknowledge the secret carried so long.

The strange story of the doctor and his wife who had had a stillborn son over thirty years before. The husband had just newly qualified, the mother was a nurse, and to them death was a part of life; the new practice was beckoning, and life had to go on. And it did. Moreover, life had been good and professional success and family joy in the shape of two healthy children had followed. But then the wife began to feel an emptiness, a hollow feeling at the centre of her being, and minor illnesses became the norm. Then dreams followed, of the baby crying out for proper recognition and burial. The mother began to make enquiries: just where had the hospital buried the stillborn in those days? She sought the help of her rabbi, a sensitive Orthodox rabbi who understood her pain and helped her in the search.

But the mother never involved her husband. After all, it was so long ago, and he saw death every day, of the young and the old, and he seemed unaffected by the past that haunted her daily life.

Until one day, when he visited a faith healer to talk of the possibility of bringing in alternative therapies to his practice. As he entered the room, she visibly paled. 'You have a dead baby on your shoulder,' she cried.

And so the burial place was identified, a plaque erected, prayers were said, the illnesses disappeared, and the baby gained its place in the family history.

More recent losses, still raw, were present as well. Babies lost at all stages of gestation or soon after birth. Orthodox, Masorti, Reform, Liberal and Progressive members, mostly women but a sprinkling of men, brought together by grief. Women now pregnant again, but needing to say goodbye to what would have been their firstborn. A couple who, despite years of treatment, had never managed to conceive, mourned the lost opportunity to form a family. (Happily, and coincidentally, a year after that first service, a daughter arrived!)

The names were read out. There was a preponderance of twins. Originally, we had added the name of baby Tabick, lost at twelve weeks gestation, because we wished to be seen as part of the congregation. But as I read the name, I remembered that awful night, the dead and numbed feeling as the baby was lost. And while the *El Malei Rahamim* was sung, asking God to guard the souls of our loved little ones, my husband came near to place his arm round my shoulder, and we wept.

All present were invited to light a memorial candle to the memory of their baby, or babies, their hopes, their dreams. The rabbis present went forward first, together with the mother, father and daughter who had first mooted the idea. There was a deep silence as the queue slowly grew, and grew. More candles had to be hastily added to the ones on the table. Time almost stood still as each person or family group came to the table, private prayers were uttered, tears spotted many a cheek, hugs were shared, and the line moved on.

Afterwards, the welcome tea and a feeling of peace. Finally, we had redeemed the memory of our babies. A Book of Memorial was inscribed and placed in the Room of Prayer at the West London Synagogue. Finally, our private tragedies had a recognized place in our rituals and synagogue life. The cry had been heard and a response from within our rich Jewish heritage had been made.

To Everything There is a Season

A Memorial Service For Our Little Ones[1]

We welcome everyone here today. A service such as this can be an emotional time for all concerned, both family and friends. We see this as part of the healing which we must all go through. We are free here, amongst friends who will understand, if we wish to grieve.

These prayers are an attempt to find a way for us to acknowledge our loss personally and within the context of the Jewish community.

After the service there will be an opportunity to write messages to be put in the Book of Remembrance.

O Eternal – I keep asking you why You allowed this to happen.
You know my anger against You.
I am confused, bitter and upset.
I cannot help it,
I am blaming You.
Why should this have happened to me?
Yet – I need You now more than ever before.
I need the comfort of knowing that, even when I cannot understand,
You still care.
Eternal, help me to trust in your love. Amen.

Anon

Psalms 121 and 23 are read.

O God,
all I feel is pain
where my baby used to be.
It was a collection of cells,
already my child, with a secret name and a secret voice.
The baby has gone and pain has settled in its place.

My hopes bled away in the night
and I am left with the pain
where my baby used to be.

Sylvia Rothschild

The Healing Song[2]
From deep within the home of my soul. Now let the healing,
the healing begin.
ana el na r'fa-na lah
Heal our bodies, open our hearts, awaken our minds,
Sh'khinah.
O Lord our God,
for a time you gave us the hope of a new life,
placed in us the expectation of a new awakening.
Now, in Your wisdom,
You have taken that hope from us,
have delayed for reasons known only to You,
the arrival of that new soul into our world.
Lord, we thank You still
for the hope you gave us.
And pray that You may renew in us that hope in time to come;
though the pain of our disappointment is real and deep,
we acknowledge still that You are our God;
You renew Life beyond Death,
You give, and take away,
You hold all our souls in the palm of Your hand.
May it be Your will to give us, once more,
the chance to share with You
in the bringing of new life to this our world;
May it be Your will that we shall be strengthened both by our
hopes and by our disappointments
and learn to love, the more deeply, that which we have.
Blessed are You, Lord, Who shares the sorrow of Your
creation.

Walter Rothschild

In the pain and fear of giving birth
I watched you come into this world
With awe and wonder in my heart.
Then I held you in my arms and cried.

In the pain and fear of impending death
I watched you go out of this world
With shock and disbelief in my heart.
Then I held you in my arms and cried.

In the pain and fear of bereavement
I've searched for you in this world
With anguish and grief in my heart.
Then I held the memory of you in my arms
. . . and cried . . . and cried.

Marylin Shaw

This has happened to us, we tell it again and again.
We pour out our hearts, full of grief.
You who are in heaven hear our prayer.
You, O Eternal, are a God of mercy and compassion.

RSGB Machzor

ana el na r'fa na lah
Heal our bodies, open our hearts, awaken our minds,
Sh'khinah.

The *T'fillah* is inserted here with the following addition in the
Sh'ma Koleinu

Hear our voice, Eternal, our God, full of mercy. Spare us and
have pity on us, and receive our prayer with love and favour.
For You are a God who listens to our prayers and needs.
Eternal, we pray for all of us present at this service that we may
know Your love and peace and hope.
Be with us, Eternal, full of compassion.
Eternal, we remember now all the babies who have died, may
they be at peace.

Be with us, Eternal, full of remembrance.
Eternal, help all parents to be aware of Your presence with them, and may they deepen their love for You, and for one another.
Be with us, Eternal, full of love.
Eternal, we thank You for all grandparents and others who have supported and encouraged us in our time of need and distress.
Be with us, Eternal, full of support and comfort.
Eternal, we thank You for all the staff in the hospitals, for their work of healing and caring and help them to progress in every area of their work.
Be with us, Eternal, full of knowledge.
Eternal, we offer You our thanks for all children and pray especially for those in any kind of need.
Be with us, Eternal, full of hope.
Eternal, bless all those who in years past lost babies and who never knew the care and support we have had.
Be with us, Eternal, full of peace.
Eternal, give us courage, trust, and above all love to face the future with hope and confidence.
Be with us, Eternal, full of creation.
Our sovereign, do not turn us away empty from Your presence, for You hear the prayers of all lips. Blessed are You Eternal, who listens to prayers.

At the end of the T'fillah *Psalm 130 is read.*

El malei rahamim
God, full of mercy
mercy-full
womb-full
Creator of all
El malei rahamim
I am emptied and hollowed
created now in Your image at this moment
empty of mercy bereft of life

angry and hurt.
The only child around is me.
El malei rahamim
shelter me under Your wings
protect me and grant me perfect rest
as I say goodbye to my unborn child
who has gone to eternity.
El malei rahamim
tahat canfei ha-Sh'khinah.
Under the wings of the *Sh'khinah* I allow my words to flow
and my cry will rend the heavens
and accompany my child
she-halkhah l'olamah
who has gone to eternity.

Sylvia Rothschild

MEMORIAL PRAYER

May God remember our babies who never had the chance of
life.

God full of compassion whose presence is over us, grant
perfect rest beneath the shelter of Your presence with the holy
and pure on high who shine as the lights of heaven, to our
loved and dear ones who have gone to their everlasting home.
Source of mercy, cover them in the shelter of Your wings for
ever and bind their soul into the gathering of life. It is God who
is their heritage. May they be at peace in their place of rest.
Amen.

Yitgadal v'yitkadash
emptiness and great separateness.
Sh'mei Rabbah
Who will know my baby's name?
Mumbling and muttering,
forcing out the blessing I stand within my community,
standing in the back row near to the door.

Tears well up and pour out
dissolving, deliquescing,
the waters of life leak out of my eyes.
Y'hei sh'lamah rabbah min shamayah.
Numbness, blessed numbness, for I shall never be complete.
V'hayyim aleinu.
The gift of life be upon us as it will never be upon my child.
Oseh shalom bimromav.
The one who makes wholeness in the highest places,
help me to live, to find it within my heart to praise You again.

Sylvia Rothschild

Kaddish and Psalm 139 are read.

All sing

Spread over us the wings of peace, shalom.
Draw water in joy from the living well
waters of life, shalom.

The Priestly Blessing.

The signing of the memorial book.[3]

A Ritual for the Loss of a Baby

Sylvia Rothschild

Gather together the parents, siblings and other family members and friends who wish to recognize and to celebrate the existence of the lost child.

Light a candle – if the ceremony takes place on Shabbat evening, an extra Shabbat candle can be used. Otherwise a *yahrzeit* candle, a commercial birthday candle, or any beautiful light can be used.

All say: בָּרוּךְ הַבָּא/בְּרוּכָה הַבָּאָה בְּשֵׁם יְיָ.
> *Barukh ha-ba/b'rukkah ha-ba'ah b'sheim Adonai,*
> *Berakhnukhem mi-beit Adonai*
> Blessed is the one who comes in the name of God, we bless you from the house of God.

Reader: We light this candle in the name of [*child's name in English and Hebrew*] whose soul has returned to God before we could properly know you. As this candle burns, so too you shone for us. As this candle flickers, so too your life was fragile; as this candle will end, so too your life has ended. Yet we knew of your existence, your light showed us a different landscape, and we will never forget what we have seen because you were, for so short a time, part of this our world.

Reader: We remember you now, we name you in our hearts. The love you brought with you remains here with us always, even though you can be neither seen nor heard. Your presence in the world was real, your leaving us is a bitter grief, all the more poignant for the brevity of your sojourn here. We remember and we will not forget. May your soul be bound up in

the ropes of eternal life, in the mesh of all who have
lived and all who will ever live.

Those present share their stories and memories of the
pregnancy and/or birth, the things they remember about the
baby. The hopes they had had, the feelings of joy and pain, the
cherished beliefs and the dawning realizations. It may be
appropriate here to create a 'book of life', or else a 'memory
box' of photographs, clothing, toys, letters and poems by
which to celebrate the life of the baby. It may be appropriate
simply to share feelings of grief and loneliness, of bewilderment and of fear for present or future siblings. It may be appropriate to acknowledge the need to say goodbye to a much
wanted child, grandchild, sibling, niece or nephew, and to
recognize all the hopes and aspirations which the child had
carried for us.

Reader: God, for a short time you entrusted to us the soul of
           [*child's name in English and Hebrew*]. For a brief
           time we had such hopes of raising a child of Israel.
           Then you took away [*child's name in English and
           Hebrew*] and with him/her you took away our hopes
           and our happiness. We now entrust to you that soul
           who is so dear to our hearts, we ask you to care for
           him/her in the enfolding wings of the *Sh'khinah*. We
           give back to you our precious child and we ask for
           your love and care for ourselves as well as for this
           child so longed for and so special. You have told us
           that as a father is tender to his children, so you will
           be tender to us. As we are unable to guide him/her
           further, we ask for you to show your mercy and
           compassion to all of us. *Av ha-Rahamim*, merciful
           Creator and Source of Life, we put our hope in you.

All: אַתָּה תִּשְׁמֹר צֵאתֵנוּ וּבוֹאֵנוּ, וּבְצֵל כְּנָפֶיךָ תַּסְתִּירֵנוּ.
           *Attah tishmor tzeiteinu u-vo'einu, u-v'tzeil
           k'nafeikha tastireinu.*
           You guard us when we go out and when we come in.
           In the shadow of your wings you shelter us.

A Ritual for the Termination of a Pregnancy

Sylvia Rothschild

Pregnancy can be ended for many reasons – all of them bring pain and distress to the people involved and no decision to end a pregnancy is ever taken lightly. This ritual is designed to cover different stages of the process: a meditation and prayer once the decision is taken; again after the termination; and finally a ritual to take the participants back into life. The liturgy is based on the understanding of the foetus as being a *rodef* – a pursuer of the life of the mother. Using the words of our matriarchs, the stories of King David, and the poetry of the Psalms, it aims to return the mother back into the cycle of life through the cycle of the new moon.

Meditation to be read silently

When David fled from his pursuer, he knew that there was but a step between himself and death. He asked, 'What have I done? What is my iniquity that I am now forced to make this choice?' And he was reassured: there was no sin that had brought about his present position. The next day was the new moon, when there was to be a feast for everyone in the household. Jonathan told David, 'You shall be missed because your seat shall be empty.' When we flee from a pursuer, we too know that there is but a step between ourselves and death. We ask ourselves, 'What have I done? What was my sin that now I must travel this road?' As Jonathan reassured David, so should we be reassured. David chose to go. Having weighed up the prospects and having considered them with his friend, he made the decision for his life. Jonathan told David to go in peace, and the Lord would be with him. For all our lives there will be someone who is missed, whose seat is vacant at family meals. Yet now we say 'Go in peace, and the Lord be with you.'

A prayer to be said by the parent of the child before the termination

To judge between life and death is to take the place of God. Yet I must make this judgment now, for a pursuer comes after me and I must act. I look to our matriarchs and ask, as did Rebecca, 'If it be so, why am I thus?' I hear the voice of God to Sarah, 'Is anything too hard for the Lord?' I hear Rachel, who said, 'God has considered me and heard my voice', I ask you God to hear me, to judge me favourably, to respond to my pain and distress. Have compassion because of Your own greatness, and because of our ancestors who trusted in You. Give me wholeness of heart so that I will love and revere you, and then I shall never lose my self-respect, nor be put to shame, for you are the power which works to save me. Look and answer me, Lord my God; lighten my eyes, lest I sleep the sleep of death. Hannah said of herself, 'I am a woman of sorrowful spirit . . . I have poured out my soul before the Lord', and she was answered, 'Go in peace, and the God of Israel grant you the petition that you have asked of Him.'[1]

To be read silently after the termination has taken place

David's child was sick, and David prayed to God for the child, he fasted and went in and lay all night upon the ground, and the elders of his house arose and went to him to raise him up from the earth, but he would not; nor would he eat bread with them. And it came to pass that the child died. David's servants were afraid to tell him that the child was dead, they feared for his reason. But when David saw that his servants whispered, he understood that the child was dead. Then he arose from the earth and washed and anointed himself and changed his clothes, and he came to the house of the Eternal and bowed down, then he came to his own house, and they set bread before him and he ate.

His servants asked him, 'What is this thing that you have done? You fasted and wept for the child while he was alive, but when the child was dead, you rose and ate bread.' And he said, 'While the child was alive I fasted and wept, for I said, "Who can tell whether God will be gracious to me?" But now that he is dead, why should I fast? Can I bring him back again? I shall go to him, but he shall not return to me.'

And David comforted Bathsheba his wife, and went in to her and lay with her, and she bore a son.[2]

Elijah arose and fled for his life, and came to Beersheba. He left his servant there and went a day's journey into wilderness, and came and sat down under a broom tree, and he asked that he might die; he said, 'It is enough now, God, take away my life, for I am not better than my ancestors.' He lay down and slept under that tree, and behold, an angel touched him and said to him, 'Arise and eat.'

He looked – and there was a cake baked on the coals, and a jar of water at his head. He ate and drank and laid himself down again.

The angel came a second time and touched him and said, 'Arise and eat; the journey is too much for you.'

And he arose and ate and drank, and journeyed. He came to a cave and lodged there, and behold the word of God came to him, 'What are you doing here, Elijah?'

. . . The Eternal passed by and a great and strong wind tore the mountains and broke the rocks in pieces, but God was not in the wind. And after the wind there was an earthquake, but God was not in the earthquake. And after the earthquake a fire, but God was not in the fire. And after the fire the sound of slender silence, a voice which asked, 'What are you doing here?'[3]

Blessed are You, God, who brings the dead to everlasting life.

בָּרוּךְ אַתָּה יְיָ מְחַיֵּה הַמֵּתִים.

Barukh ata Adonai m'hayyeh ha-meitim

May my child come to his/her resting place in peace.

עַל מְקוֹמוֹ יָבֹא בְשָׁלוֹם/עַל מְקוֹמָהּ תָּבֹא בְשָׁלוֹם.

Al m'komo yavo v'shalom/ Al m'komah tavo v'shalom

A prayer to be said after the termination

Be gracious to me, God, for I am in distress; my eye is consumed with grief, my soul and my body. My life is spent with grief, my strength fails, I am like a broken vessel. Let me not be ashamed, God, for I have called on you. I said in my haste, 'I am cut off from before Your eyes,' but still you heard the voice of my entreaties when I cried to You. There are those who say that God has forsaken me. God, do not be far from me and make haste to help me. Restore me back to life, bring me back from the depths of the earth. You are my hope, You have searched me and known me, You are acquainted with all my ways. Out of the depths I cry to You, O God, hear my voice. How long shall I take counsel in my soul, having sorrow in my heart daily? How long will you hide Your face from me? As for me I will behold Your face in righteousness. I will be satisfied when I awake, beholding Your likeness.[4]

A candle is lit each evening for seven days after the termination and the verses recited:

'For you will light my candle, the Eternal my God will lighten my darkness.'

   'Go in peace, and God be with you.'

   'Be of good courage and let your heart be strong, all you who hope in the Lord.'[5]

On the evening of the seventh day, there should be a meal with close family and friends, after which the mother could pray the traditional prayer of the person who has recovered from illness.[6]

Or: 'I thank You, Lord my God and God of my ancestors, God of the spirits of all flesh. You were with me in the time of my affliction, and You helped me. In time of trouble You showed me the path of life, and the fullness of joy. You showed me the sweetness which is at your right hand for ever.

בָּרוּךְ אַתָּה יְיָ אֱלֹהֵינוּ מֶלֶךְ הָעוֹלָם הַגּוֹמֵל לְחַיָּבִים טוֹבוֹת שֶׁגְּמָלַנִי כָּל־טוֹב.

Barukh attah Adonai, eloheinu melekh ha-olam, ha-gomel l'hayyavim tovot, she-g'malani kol tov

Blessed are you Lord our God, sovereign of the universe, who shows favour to the undeserving, and has shown me great favour.

מִי שֶׁגְּמָלְךָ כָּל־טוֹב הוּא יִגְמָלֵךְ כָּל־טוֹב.

All respond: '*Mi she-g'malakh kol tov, hu yig'm'leikh kol tov*

May God who has shown favour to you, continue to favour you with all that is good.'[7]

The following paragraph from the Amidah may be recited:

'Heal us and we shall be healed; save us and we shall be saved, for it is You we praise. Send relief and healing for all our illnesses, our sufferings and our wounds. For you are a merciful and faithful healer.

בָּרוּךְ אַתָּה יְיָ רוֹפֵא הַחוֹלִים

Barukh attah Adonai rofei ha-holim

Blessed are You God, who heals the sick.'

A prayer to be said thirty days after the termination

O Eternal my God, I cried to you and you have healed me. You have brought my soul from Sheol; you have kept me alive, that I should not go down to the pit. Give thanks to God's holy name, for his anger lasts but a moment; His favour is for a lifetime; weeping may endure for a night, but joy comes in the morning.

My child, my pursuer, is no more. You, who see the unformed substance, who knows each person made in secret, hide him under the shadow of your wings. Be gracious to us both. I cannot bring him back. One day I shall go to him, but he shall not return to me. I have been into the wilderness alone, too distraught to eat or drink, not able to notice the life-giving sources around me. I have made my journey, have touched Sheol, been buffeted by the strong winds of my emotions, and the earthquakes of my soul, and now I know the voice of slender silence asks me, 'What am I doing here now?'

David arose and comforted Bathsheba. I now comfort others and am comforted by them. And I ask you, in the words of the psalmist: Let me be 'like a tree planted by the rivers of water, that brings forth its fruit in its season; its leaf also shall not wither; and whatever it does shall prosper'.[8]

God, the soul you gave to my child was pure, for You created it, You formed it, and breathed it into the body. You care for the soul for ever, taking it to everlasting life.

On the Rosh Hodesh following the thirty-day marker, it is recommended that the mother immerse herself in the Mikveh, and recite Psalm 51.

Be kind to me, God, in Your mercy,
in Your great compassion blot out my misdeeds.
Wash me free from my guilt and cleanse me from my sin.
For my misdeeds I know too well, and my sin is always before me.
Against You, You only, have I sinned, and done what is evil in Your sight.
Therefore You are just in Your sentence, and right in your judgment
But even though I was born to err, and my mother conceived me in sin;
the truth is still what You desire within me,
and in my inmost heart You show me wisdom.
Purify me with hyssop, and I shall be clean,
wash me and I shall be whiter than snow.
Let me hear joy and gladness, so that the bones You crushed dance again.
Turn Your gaze away from my sins, and blot out all my guilt.

Create a pure heart for me, God, and put a firm and steadfast spirit in me.

Do not cast me away from Your presence, nor take Your holy spirit from me.

Give me back the joy of Your salvation and let a willing spirit uphold me.

Then I will teach transgressors the way, so that sinners may return to You.

Keep me from bloodshed, God, You are the God who saves me.

My tongue shall ring out Your justice,

God, open my lips and my mouth shall declare Your praise.

For You desire no sacrifice, or I would give it,

burned offerings you do not want.

God's sacrifices are a humbled spirit;

a broken and contrite heart you will not despise.

Into Your hand, God, I commend the spirit of my child.

The Eternal One is with me, I shall not fear.

בְּיָדְךָ נַפְקִיד רוּחַת בְּנִי יְיָ לִי וְלֹא אִירָה.

B'yad'kha nafkid ruhat b'ni, Adonai li, lo ira.

Living Infertility

A Memorial Service to Mark Lives That Weren't and the Life That Is

Harriett Goldenberg and
Elizabeth Tikvah Sarah

Background

The background and context to this piece has three dimensions: the personal experience of an individual Jewish woman living with infertility; the exclusion of the experience of Jewish women in general – and the experience of childless Jewish women in particular – from the conceptual framework and rituals of rabbinic Judaism – and the related assumption that in/fertility is a 'women's' issue; the friendship of two women – one a woman living with infertility and the other a rabbi who is both a lesbian and childless – and their collaboration in creating a Jewish ritual to mark the experience of infertility.

Harriett Goldenberg: *A Jewish woman living with infertility*

Two nights before my wedding my sister held a party in her home. Sitting on the steps with my best friend, I saw the path ahead of me very clearly – you get married, you have children, you grow old and you die. I was about to step on to the first rung of the ladder. Four years later, when the recognition of infertility began, I unwillingly took the first step off that ladder.

Infertility takes you outside the life-cycle, and equally significant and painful for me, it takes you outside the mainstream Jewish world.

One of the most heart-rending aspects of my experience of infertility has been the implications for my relationship with Judaism and the Jewish community, to this day a struggle not resolved.

'Thou shalt be fruitful and multiply' (Gen. 1.28). It is a commandment. By virtue of my infertility I was going against the precepts of my faith. Biblical Judaism, through the characters of Sarah, Rebecca, Rachel and Hannah, makes it clear that if God shines his light upon you, you will bear children. And if he doesn't? What does that mean? Where does that leave you? Jewish liturgy offers no solace to the infertile woman; only condemnation.

For me, the process of infertilty involved a loss of innocence and a frightening recognition of impending marginality. In the early days it was my inclination to speak to a rabbi, to turn to a rabbi, for what I did not know. Answers to the mystery, I suppose; how was I to understand what was happening to my life? Of course there were no religious or spiritual answers that could be offered, only warmth and compassion. But the questions and the anguish remained.

The history of my infertility actually charts the friendship between Elli Sarah and myself. Having spoken to one rabbi already, I was left unsatisfied, and then at a Reform conference I was struck by the fact that I was surrounded by rabbis – someone must be able to help me. A friend suggested I spoke to Elli. I knew Elli already, but not well. Initially I balked at the suggestion. By virtue of being a lesbian, Elli was marginal. That was not what I wanted. What I wanted was to work out how not to step outside the mainstream community. In fact I did speak to Elli, and while there were still no answers to be offered, she conveyed a deep sense of understanding that was of great value to me.

That conversation probably marked the beginning of the long road to discovery of the courage to forge ahead with a life that doesn't fit; a life I have had to shape myself without benefit of religious or communal frameworks.

Elizabeth Tikvah Sarah: *Rabbinic Judaism and the exclusion of women*

Jewish feminists have been making the point – in various ways – for a quarter of a century now, that Jewish women are marginalized/rendered 'other' in Jewish life – both in 'theory' and in 'practice' (for example, see the ground-breaking anthologies: Koltun, 1976 – especially articles by Greenberg, Hyman, Plaskow, Geller and Kolton; Heschel, 1983 – especially articles by Adler, Bauman, Ozick and Plaskow). But – by definition – these are 'other' voices. And the immense expansion in Jewish feminist research and publications in the past two decades (see especially: Adler, 1998; Alpert, 1997; Biale, 1984; Grossman and Haut, 1993; Hauptman, 1998; Peskowitz and Levitt, 1997; Plaskow, 1991; Sheridan, 1994) has not changed this reality. We are still living in the era of male-defined 'rabbinic Judaism'. And so in his book *Covenant of Blood. Circumcision and Gender in Rabbinic Judaism* (1996), Lawrence Hoffman adds the male voice of authority to the case. On the basis of a painstaking analysis of rabbinic texts, Hoffman argues that the early rabbis' halakhic approach is framed by their preoccupation with the perpetuation of the Jewish 'male lifeline' (25, 81) and the exclusive role of Jewish males in controlling and transforming 'wild' 'nature' in the interests of 'culture' (165–7). While Jewish females are defined from birth by their biological destiny as bearers of children, Jewish males are marked out from eight days old onwards as the bearers of Jewish culture: the culturally controlled blood-letting involved in *b'rit milah* (the covenant of circumcision) – by contrast with the natural blood-flows that characterize menstruation and child-birth – expressing the different destinies of the two sexes imposed by the system of rabbinic Judaism.

And so, now it's official: rabbinic Judaism is defined by a

patriarchal agenda: the triumph of culture over nature; the exclusion of Jewish females from Jewish culture; and the ritualization of the male lifeline – not only through *b'rit milah*, but also through *bar mitzvah* – when thirteen-year-old males become obligated to perform 610 of the 613 commandments (three commandments being set aside as female obligations: Shabbat/festival candles, dividing the *challah* dough and *niddah* – maintaining the laws of ritual purity) – and *kiddushin*, Jewish marriage – involving the 'acquisition' (*kinyan*) of the bride by the groom. Since the purpose of Jewish marriage is reproduction and the continuation of the 'male lifeline' is dependent upon it, it is clear that the marking of Jewish males as the bearers of Jewish culture and 'controllers' of nature may involve a suppression and denial of their own biological nature and experience of in/fertility.

The implications of the dualistic patriarchal approach to Jewish males and females are immense and complex – and at least two outcomes are axiomatic as far as Jewish females are concerned: the identity of Jewish females lies in their biological destiny as child-bearers (either potential or actual); the lives of Jewish females are significant solely in the context of their role in maintaining and nurturing the male lifeline. Women who do not bear children, women who live independently of men, exist on the margins of rabbinic Judaism. And yet, these Jewish women exist. And now, some Jewish women – both with and without partners and children – are rabbis.

Harriett Goldenberg: *A Jewish woman deciding to mark her infertility by creating her own Jewish ritual*

Ritual is a concrete and possibly public declaration or marker of a significant event. In the case of infertility, that event is a loss. It is this concretizing that is potentially helpful in the process of addressing infertility, which by its very nature is often intangible. While a ceremony does not and cannot take away the loss, it can provide important acknowledgment and respect for the reality of the experience.

The germ of the idea of a ritual to mark my infertility and childlessness actually began one year during the *Yizkor* (memorial) service on Yom Kippur. While saying *kaddish* for my father, I suddenly realized that I wasn't simply saying *kaddish* for him, but for my children, for five children that hadn't come to be (through five failed attempts at *in vitro* fertilization). The recognition was overwhelming.

But being a private person who balks at the notion of 'melodrama', it took another two years before I put the idea into action. What would be the value of a ritual? I had a lot of encouragement from friends, which I actually experienced as an expression of their deep concern and desperation for me to find a mechanism with which to put the subject to rest. But I knew a ceremony wasn't going to be some sort of magic potion; it wasn't going to take the pain away; in fact, it wasn't going to change anything, so what was the point?

Within Judaism there are rituals and prayers to mark everything from the sighting of a rainbow to the opening of a meeting. Where there is a death there is a funeral. It is a social, religious and 'legal' given. But for the infertile there are no such givens. It was when I began to see a memorial service as an act of respect, an entitlement and a way of bringing my experience into Judaism that I began to appreciate its value, and to feel that it was something I wanted to go ahead with. It was potentially a way of giving myself something I had longed for, recognition of the fact that I was a Jewish woman with this experience, rather than a woman whose life experience took her outside Judaism.

Elizabeth Tikvah Sarah: *Re-creating Jewish ritual and creating a new model for rabbinic practice*

So, what happens when a Jewish woman living with infertility chooses to lay claim to Judaism on her own terms? What happens when a rabbi, who is also a lesbian and childless, chooses to re-shape rabbinic concerns from the perspective of her own female experience and model a new way of working rabbinically? And when they decide to collaborate together, what then? In fact, the coming together of those two perspectives linked by deep understanding and a strong friendship was a crucial factor. It was an important event for us both, both of us bringing our courage and need to expand religious parameters. Harriett claims that she would not have gone ahead if she had had to do it alone. The collaboration actually signified having a partner in a process that had largely been very lonely.

A woman rabbi at work

While a lone woman rabbi – Regina Jonas – was ordained in Germany in 1935 (Sarah, 1994a; 1995), it is less than thirty years since women *rabbis* began to work within Jewish communities around the world (Sheridan, 1994). Women rabbis are rabbis who are women – and for some their gender is incidental. Women rabbis have also transformed rabbinic practice with their experience and their concerns as women – and for some women rabbis, their awareness of women's issues, in general, and commitment to feminism, in theory and practice, has also had an impact on their ways of working as rabbis (Geller, 1983; Sarah, 1994b).

My approach to rabbinic work was shaped by my engagement with the Women's Liberation Movement in Britain in the late 1970s. So when I embarked on rabbinic training at the Leo Baeck College in London in 1984, I was already committed to bringing my experience as a woman and as a lesbian and my feminist perspective with me into the rabbinate. Since space does not allow a fuller treatment of this nexus, I want to focus on one aspect of it which has direct bearing on my collaboration with Harriett: I see my rabbinic role – whether I'm teaching, praying, singing, counselling, visiting or facilitating a ritual – in terms of being *an enabler*. Women have always been the 'enablers' in Jewish life (Greenberg, 1976) – enabling Jewish boys and men and girls to assume their prescribed roles.

Nothing new about that. But when the enabler is a rabbi, something changes. An enabling rabbi is someone who – through sharing her learning, skills and experience – enables other Jews to be Jews and to do Jewishly in the ways they choose. This is what I try to do. Of course, it's not quite as simple as that. It involves acknowledging my power as a rabbi – and the fact that my role has an 'official' dimension (which includes 'external' sanctions and regulations), recognizing the projections of others – which are influenced by their past experiences and their own needs – and trying to create a bridge between my world as a rabbi and the world of another Jew which both of us can cross. So I don't don clerical dress or engage in any of the other behaviour – such as making an entrance into the midst of an 'upstanding' congregation – which emphasize my rabbinic 'status'. At the same time I don't pretend that five years rabbinic training combined with eleven years rabbinic working experience doesn't put me in a special situation. What I try to do is draw on my specialized skills to enable other Jews to take control of their own Jewish lives.

Working with Harriett: A case in point

Harriett and I are friends. I am not 'Harriett's rabbi'. When Harriett talked to me about 'marking' her infertility and working with me to create a ritual, she made it clear that she wanted the support of a friend and the specialized input of a friend who is also a rabbi. I didn't tell Harriett what she should or shouldn't include. I asked her why she wanted a ritual and what she was hoping to express through it. We discussed her experience both of her infertility and of Jewish rituals – particularly those associated with death. We reflected together on what made a Jewish ritual Jewish. I identified some texts and materials she might want to look at. We exchanged readings and ideas. We shared our experiences of marginality within the Jewish community. We talked about who she would like to be involved – and where and when she would like the ritual to take place. We discussed my role in the ritual. We considered the 'befores' and 'afters' – as well as the content of the ritual. Harriett made choices and decisions.

Having helped to shape Harriett's ritual, when it came to the event itself, I saw myself primarily as a friend sitting with her in a circle of friends; as a friend sitting next to her and giving her the practical support to move the ritual from stage to stage, and the moral support to do it for herself. Apart from that, my explicit 'rabbinic' contribution involved singing Debbie Friedman's *Mi She – beirakh* and the memorial prayer, *El malei rahamim*. A number of friends made particular contributions to the ritual. We also sang and read and sat in silence together.

Harriett Goldenberg: *A memorial service to mark lives that weren't and the life that is*

Preparations

Having decided to go ahead with the ceremony, it was important to find a date when everyone I wanted to attend could be there. This was not a funeral. I could not expect that people would make great alterations to their own arrangements to attend on short notice. It was also important that I invited them myself; that was part of the process of acknowledging 'I am really going to do this'. I chose Sunday, 1 September, which was just prior to the Rosh Hashanah period, the end of the year, and the end of a ten-year era for me, perhaps. As it happened, everyone I invited was able to attend, which signified for me the respect and importance they attributed to the event. In fact, some thanked me for inviting them. Elli was of course, the first person I approached both to help me in preparing the ceremony and to be by my side on the day. The day decided upon, we began preparing the service itself.

The ceremony must have been brewing inside me for some time, because creating the service was actually a very simple process that evolved with great ease. The Jewish funeral service formed the basis for the ceremony. Elli was particularly helpful in making the appropriate alterations to the prayers to convey that this was a ceremony to mark lives that were never to be. Coming from our different, but very complementary professional backgrounds, we both had a clear sense of the appropriate rhythm. I knew that there needed to be a combination of elements: music, personal statements, the *kaddish*, solemnity and joy. This was a ceremony to mark the lives that weren't, but also to acknowledge the life that is – that is mine. Having decided on all the elements, and having enlisted the relevant people to take part, we then prepared the written ceremony, and made copies for everyone.

Again, as with a funeral service, I wanted to have a quiet gathering after the ceremony and, modelled on a funeral, people volunteered to bring dry cakes.

On the morning of the day, I laid out the chairs in the garden, arranged the dining table, and organized the tape recorder in the house. The truth is, because of who I am, the practicalities came very easily. The emotional process was a different matter. A friend rang early in the morning of the day of the service, and even at that late stage, I was still asking myself whether I was doing the right thing. Finally, I told myself, that *they*, my longed-for children, deserved a mark of respect and that was that.

The time came, everyone arrived, and we began the ceremony. After the ceremony we gathered in the house over tea and cakes, and there was very easy and warm chat. People left about an hour later. Kindly, Elli and her partner Cathy invited me to come for dinner, which was the perfect conclusion to the day.

A Memorial Service to Mark Lives That Weren't
And The Life That Is

Created by Harriett Goldenberg and Elli Tikvah Sarah

SUNDAY I SEPTEMBER 1996 – 14 ELUL 5756

Setting

A group of thirteen intimate friends sat on chairs formed in a circle, in the garden. Each person's presence had particular meaning for Harriett, but the fact that there was a *minyan* (10 adults) was also important. Elli and Harriett sat beside each other. On the other side of Harriett was a small table with a *yahrzeit* (memorial) candle and matches. Everyone had copies of the prepared ceremony.

The ceremony

The song 'Soft' by Chuck Mangione, coming from the open doors of the house.

A friend offered some of her own thoughts, having been alongside the process of infertility treatment and the subsequent years of struggle.

Psalm 23 – a psalm of David (translated into English by Elli, read together)

> The Eternal is my shepherd
> I shall not want
> In green fields You let me lie
> by quiet streams You lead me,
> restoring my soul.
> Guiding me in paths of truth
> for such is your name.
> Though I walk through the valley
> of the shadow of death
> I fear no harm
> for You are beside me;
> Your rod and staff
> they comfort me.

You spread a table before me
in front of my enemies.
You soothe my head with oil;
my cup runs over.
Surely goodness and mercy seek me
all the days of my life,
and I shall dwell in the house of the Eternal
for ever.

Oyfn Pripetshok (by Mark Warshowsky, from the Reform
Mahzor, Harriett's father's favourite song, a song she has
known all her life – sung together in Yiddish):

oyfn pripetshok brent a fayerl,
Un in shtub iz heys
Under rebe lernt klyne kinderlech
Dem alef beys.

Zet-zhe kinderlech, gedenkt-zhe tayere,
Vos ir lernt do;
Zogt-zhe noch amol, an take noch amol;
Komets – alef: O!

Lernt Kinder, mit groys cheyshek,
Azoy zog gicher fun aych kenen ivre,
Der bukumt a fon.

Lernt Kinder, hot nic moyre,
Yeder onhoyb iz shver,
Gliklech der vos hot gelernt toyre,
Tsi darf der mensh noch mer?

Ir vet kinder, elter vern,
Vet ir aleyn farshteyn
Vifil in di oyses lign trern,
Un vifil geveyn.

Az ir vet kinder, dem goles shlepn,
Oysgemutshet zayn,
Zolt ir fun di oysyes koyech shepn,
Kukt in zey arayn!

On the little hearth a fire is burning bright,
The schoolroom is so warm –
The old teacher's telling all the children there
How the alphabet was born.

Listen children, listen precious ones,
Listen to our lore,
But first you have to read the ancient alphabet
Before you can learn more.

It will lead you to the holy books,
Remember what I say –
Then I'll give a banner to the best of you
On the holiday.

Pay attention, children, listen well,
It's always hard to start –
Happy is the man who lives with knowledge,
Takes learning to his heart.

When you'll grow up to be men some day,
Then you'll surely know,
How full of human tears is our old alphabet,
How full of trials and woes.

And if one day, we should be driven out
From this land of pain –
May you seek and find in our old alphabet
the strength to build again.

For Strong Women (by Marge Piercy – Harriett's favourite
poem, read by a friend)

A strong woman is a woman who is straining
A strong woman is a woman standing
on tiptoe and lifting a barbell
while trying to sing Boris Godunov
A strong woman is a woman at work
and while she shovels, she talks about
how she doesn't mind crying, it opens

the ducts of the eyes, and throwing up
develops the stomach muscles, and
she goes on shovelling with tears
in her nose.

A strong woman is a woman in whose head
a voice is repeating, I told you so,
ugly, bad girl, bitch, nag, shrill, witch,
ballbuster, nobody will ever love you back,
why aren't you feminine, why aren't
you soft, why aren't you quiet, why
aren't you dead?

A strong woman is a woman determined
to do something others are determined
not to be done. She is pushing up on the bottom
of a lead coffin lid. She is trying to raise
a manhole cover with her head, she is trying
to butt her way through a steel wall.
Her head hurts. People waiting for the hole
to be made say, Hurry, you're so strong.

A strong woman is a woman bleeding
inside. A strong woman is a woman making
herself strong every morning while her teeth
loosen and her back throbs. Every baby,
a tooth, midwives used to say, and now
every battle a scar. A strong woman
is a mass of scar tissue that aches
when it rains and wounds that bleed
when you bump them, and memories that get up
in the night and clump in boots to and fro.

A strong woman is a woman who craves love
like oxygen or she turns blue choking.
A strong woman is a woman who loves
strongly and weeps strongly and is strongly
terrified and has strong needs. She is strong in words, in
action, in connection, in feeling;

she is not strong as a stone but as a wolf
suckling her young. Strength is not in her
but she enacts it as a wind fills a sail.

What comforts her is others loving
her equally for the strength and for the weakness
from which it issues, lightning from the cloud.
Lightning stuns. In rain, the clouds disperse.
Only water of connection remains,
flowing through us. Strong is what we make
each other. Until we are all strong together,
a strong woman is a woman strongly afraid.

Kol Ha'olam kullo *(sung together)*

Kol ha'olam kullo gesher tzar m'od, veha'ikar lo l'facheid klal
The whole world is a very narrow bridge, but the essential
thing is never to be afraid (*Rabbi Nahman of Bratzlav*).

A personal statement of validation from another friend

*Mi she-beirakh (sung by Elli) – composed by Debbie
Friedman.*

Mi she-beirakh Avoteinu, m'kor ha-b'rakhah le-imoteinu
May the One who blessed our fathers, the fountain of blessing
for our mothers,
May the source of strength who blessed the ones before us,
help us find the courage to make our lives a blessing. And let us
say: Amen.
Mi she-beirakh Imoteinu, m'kor ha-b'rakhah la-avoteinu.
May the One who blessed our mothers, the fountain of blessing for our fathers,
Bless those in need of healing with *r'fuah sh'leimah* (complete
healing), the renewal of body, the renewal of spirit. And let us
say: Amen.

Light candle (Harriett)

My Children (a poem written and said by Harriett)

I miss you
you who were to be – whatever and whoever you would have
been
I miss you
you who aren't and will never be
The part of me that's never been
The part of me I shall never meet and will miss and long for,
for ever
I miss your life and I miss my life – as I thought it would be
Something has ended that never had a chance to begin
And I'll miss you and the mother I was to be, for ever.

El Malei Rahamim *(adapted and sung by Elli, then read collectively)*

God full of compassion, whose presence is over us, grant perfect rest beneath the shelter of your presence with the holy and pure on high who shine as the lights of heaven, to the beginning of lives who have gone to their everlasting home. Master of mercy, cover them in the shelter of your wings for ever, and bind their souls into the gathering of life. It is the Eternal One who is their heritage. May they be at peace in their place of rest. Amen.

Kaddish (said by Harriett, responses said collectively)

Let us magnify and let us sanctify in this world the great name of God whose will created it. May God's kingdom come in your lifetime, and in your days, and in the lifetime of the family of Israel – quickly and speedily may it come. Amen.

May the greatness of God's being be blessed from eternity to eternity.

Let us bless and let us extol, let us tell aloud and let us raise aloft, let us set on high and let us honour, let us exalt and let us praise the Holy One, whose name be blessed, who is far beyond any blessing or song, any honour or any consolation that can be spoken in this world. Amen.

May great peace from heaven and the gift of life be granted to us and to all the family of Israel. Amen.

May the Maker of peace in the highest bring this peace upon us and upon all Israel. Amen.

Silence – quiet; then move into house for tea and dry cakes.

Harriett Goldenberg: *Reflections after the event*

All I can say is that it was as it should have been. As well as marking my childlessness, what *isn't*, the ceremony also marked what *is* . . . I felt surrounded by a circle of love and in a way that I cannot fully explain or understand, it left me with a sense of warmth and peacefulness. The pain of childlessness will be with me always, incorporated now into who I am. The ceremony did not, and as I already knew could not, change that. But it was the right thing to do. In addition, I know that it had great meaning for those who were there with me. It took courage both in a personal and public sense to create the ceremony. My hope would be that for others it would become a given, a marker of one of the tragedies of the life cycle. This particular service with its very personal elements and resonances is clearly offered only as a model of what might take place. Creating it myself, albeit very much together with a very close friend who happens to be a rabbi, was a valuable act of reclaiming dignity and recognition as a Jewish woman in the Jewish world.

Three years later it is still my relationship with Judaism, with my God, that troubles me, the mysteries that we don't get answers to.

Passed Over (Harriett Goldenberg, 4 April 1999)

And the angel of death . . .
but what of the angel of life – passed over
I've been passed over – squeezed out
young moms on one side,
mothers, grandmothers to be, on the other,
the children I didn't have about to become

parents themselves
squeezed out – invisible
the agony and the torture of watching life.
The cycles repeat themselves as they should
born out of sync to live a life out of sync
relegated to the bleechers with a box of handkerchiefs
be gracious and serene – auntie Harriett – everyone's best
friend, no one's mother
unfortunately the knife in your heart
won't kill you.
There's a long time life to go – how many more
generations to watch from the sidelines?
Give me a cross to bear any day over this.
'Being a woman is a disability, like being blind or crippled,'
the orthodox rabbi said
not true
but a woman who isn't a woman
well, you've got something there!
Very cruel.
I'll go up in a puff of smoke one day
and that will be that – for eternity.
'There ya go', as they say.
Is there a punchline somewhere?

References

Adler, Rachel, 1998. *Engendering Judaism. An Inclusive Theology and Ethics*, Philadelphia: The Jewish Publication Society

—, 1983. 'The Jew Who Wasn't There: Halakhah and the Jewish Woman', in Susannah Heschel (ed.), *On Being A Jewish Feminist. A Reader*, New York: Schocken Books

Alpert, Rebecca, 1997. *Like Bread on the Seder Plate. Jewish Lesbians and the Transformation of Tradition*, New York: Columbia University Press

Bauman, Batya, 1983. 'Women-Identified Women In Male-Identified Judaism', in Susanna Heschel (ed.), *On Being a Jewish Feminist. A Reader*, New York: Schocken Books

Biale, Rachel, 1984. *Women and Jewish Law. An Exploration of Women's Issues in Halakhic Sources*, New York: Schocken Books

Blue, Lionel and Jonathan Magonet (eds), 1985. *Days of Awe*, Forms of Prayer, Vol. III, London: Reform Synagogues of Great Britain

Geller, Laura, 1983. 'Reflections to a Woman Rabbi', in Susanna Heschel (ed.), *On Being a Jewish Feminist. A Reader*, New York: Schocken Books

Gold, Michael, 1998. *And Hannah Wept. Infertility, Adoption and the Jewish Couple*, Philadelphia: The Jewish Publication Society

Goldenberg, Harriett, 1997a. 'The Place of Ritual as a Marker of Infertility', *The Journal of Infertility Counselling*, Vol. 4, No. 1, 8–9

—, 1997b. 'Who am I if I am not a Mother?', in Simon du Plock (ed.), *Case Studies in Existential Psychotherapy and Counselling*, Chichester: Wiley and Son

Greenberg, Blu, 1976. 'Judaism and Feminism', in Elizabeth Koltan (ed.), *The Jewish Woman. New Perspectives*, New York: Schocken Books

Grossman, Susan and Rivka Haut, 1993. *Daughters of the King. Women and the Synagogue*, Philadelphia: The Jewish Publication Society.

Hauptman, Judith, 1998. *Rereading the Rabbis. A Woman's Voice*, Oxford: Westview Press

Hoffman, Lawrence, 1996. *Covenant of Blood. Circumcision and Gender in Rabbinic Judaism*, Chicago and London: The University of Chicago Press

Hyman, Paula, 1976. 'The Other Half Women in the Jewish Tradition', in Elizabeth Koltan (ed.), *The Jewish Woman. New Perspectives*, New York: Schocken Books

Ozick, Cynthia, 1983. 'Notes toward Finding the Right Question', in Susannah Heschel (ed.), *On Being A Jewish Feminist. A Reader*, New York: Schocken Books

Peskowitz, Miriam and Laura Levitt (eds), 1997. *Judaism Since Gender*, New York: Routledge

Piercy, Marge, 1995. *Eight Chambers of the Heart*, London: Penguin Books

Plaskow, Judith, 1991. *Standing Again At Sinai. Judaism from a Feminist Perspective*, HarperSanFrancisco

—, 1983. 'The Right Question is Theological', in Susannah Heschel (ed.), *On Being A Jewish Feminist. A Reader*, New York: Schocken Books

Resnick, Elizabeth Levine (ed.), *A Ceremonies Sampler: New Rites, Celebrations and Observances of Jewish Women*, San Diego, CA: Institute for Continuing Jewish Education

Sarah, Elizabeth, 1995. 'The Discovery of Fräulein Rabbiner Regina Jonas: Making Sense of Our Inheritance', *European Judaism*, 95:2, Autumn

—, 1994a. 'Rabbi Regina Jonas, 1902–1944: Missing Link in a Broken Chain', in Sybil Sheridan (ed.), *Hear Our Voice. Women Rabbis Tell Their Stories*, London: SCM Press 1994

—, 1994b. 'Who We Are – An Introduction', in ibid.

Sheridan, Sybil 1994. Ed., *Hear Our Voice. Women Rabbis Tell Their Stories*, London: SCM Press

Relationships and Change

Prayers Surrounding Marriage

Alexandra Wright

A Prayer to recite on one's engagement

The agreement to marry in Jewish tradition was taken very seriously. The Western concept of 'engagement' as we know it did not exist in ancient times. Instead, a ceremony named *T'naim* (conditions) enacted the setting-out of the date and financial conditions of the marriage of a woman and man.

The following prayer is not for the ceremony of *T'naim*, which involved the writing out of the conditions and the *kinyan* (the formal acceptance of the contract). These words, which can be recited by the couple, either privately or publicly, acknowledge that a couple may wish to have a period of time in which to prepare themselves for marriage, to allow their two families to become familiar with each other and to take that first ritual step celebrating their love and forthcoming union that leads to marriage.

> Upon my bed at night
> I sought him whom my soul loves;
> I sought him, but found him not;
> I called him, but he gave no answer.
> 'I will rise now and go about the city,
> in the streets and in the squares;
> I will seek him whom my soul loves.'
> I sought him, but found him not.
> The sentinels found me,
> as they went about in the city.
> 'Have you seen him whom my soul loves?'
> Scarcely had I passed them,
> when I found him whom my soul loves.
> I held him, and would not let him go
> until I brought him into my mother's house . . . (Song of Songs 3.1–4)

I rejoice in my happiness, O God,
My soul exults with joy.
You have blessed me with love and companionship,
With the affection and friendship of one whom my soul
loves.
Guide me, O God, as I enter this new part of my life.
Help me to acknowledge the loss of being single and free,
And to understand that in this new relationship, my free-
dom acquires a different aspect.
I am enriched, and my consciousness is deepened by this
love.
Help me as I bring him into the house of my mother and
father.
May they see my happiness and the qualities I see in him.
May I be gentle and giving in the months that lie ahead,
Tender and kind as we shape the beginning of our marriage.

Loving God, may Your steadfast love and faithfulness
always be with us,
May we be guided by Your righteousness and peace.
Trusting in You, Eternal God,
May we learn to trust each other and be strengthened by this
happiness
And the blessings of love and companionship. Amen.

Awakening on the day of one's marriage

נָכוֹן לִבִּי אֱלֹהִים נָכוֹן לִבִּי אָשִׁירָה וַאֲזַמֵּרָה: עוּרָה כְבוֹדִי עוּרָה הַנֵּבֶל וְכִנּוֹר אָעִירָה
שָׁחַר:

My heart is ready, O God, my heart is ready. I shall sing and
play music; Awake my soul, awake O harp and lyre, I shall
awake at dawn. I will give thanks to you, Eternal God, among
all peoples, I will sing praises to you among the nations (Psalm
57.8–9).

נָתַתָּה שִׂמְחָה בְלִבִּי מֵעֵת דְּגָנָם וְתִירוֹשָׁם רָבּוּ:
אוֹדְךָ אֲדֹנָי אֱלֹהַי בְּכָל־לְבָבִי וַאֲכַבְּדָה שִׁמְךָ לְעוֹלָם:

You have put into my heart such happiness, more than others

had from grain and wine. Therefore, I thank You Eternal One my God with all my heart, and glorify your name for ever (Psalm 4.8; 86.12)

תַּעְטְנֵי אוֹר כַּשַׂלְמָה אֶחֱסֶה בְסֵתֶר בְּנָפֶיךָ: גַּם-צִפּוֹר מָצְאָה בַיִת וּדְרוֹר קֵן לָהּ
אֲשֶׁר-שָׁתָה אֶפְרֹחֶיהָ אָז בְּאַהֲבָתִי מָצָאתִי מִקְדָּשִׁי כִּי: דּוֹדִי לִי וַאֲנִי לוֹ וְעָלַי תְּשׁוּקָתוֹ:

You enfold me in your robe of light, I take shelter beneath the wings of Your presence. Even as the sparrow finds a home and the swallow has her nest, so in this love have I found my sanctuary, for I am my beloved's and my beloved is mine, And his longing is all for me (Psalms 104.2; 61.5; 84.4; Song of Songs 2.16; 7.11).

Soon we shall come together, the bride and the groom, beneath the intimate shelter of the *huppah*.
As love and faithfulness clasp each other, justice and peace embrace, so shall we encompass each other with our love.

Purify my heart, O God, as I enter the intimate chamber of marriage; have mercy on me according to your steadfast love; according to your abundant mercy blot out my transgressions. Wash me thoroughly from my iniquity, and cleanse me from my sin. You desire truth in the inward being; therefore teach me wisdom in my secret heart. Purge me with hyssop and I shall be clean; wash me, and I shall be whiter than snow.

As I prepare to enter this covenant of affection and truth, I praise You, O God, who created joy and happiness, bridegroom and bride, love and companionship, peace and friendship. In the quietness of this moment, protect me, My God, and reach out to me with tenderness. I turn to You, trusting in Your faithful love and in the joy of your salvation. Amen.

A b'deken *ceremony*

There is some debate about the source of the *b'deken* ceremony. Is it the act of veiling the bride before the ceremony of marriage, or is it the act of the groom lifting the bride's veil just

prior to the marriage blessings? Both have their origins in the
Bible. When Rebecca is brought to Isaac for the first time by
Abraham's servant, she veils herself, an act perhaps symbolic
of modesty and dignity. Jacob, on the other hand, was tricked
by his father-in-law into marrying Leah instead of Rachel. The
act of lifting the veil allows the groom to check that the bride is
the right woman! Whatever the origins, *b'deken* became an
important part of the preparations for marriage. It was called
hakhnasat ha-kallah la-huppah – 'bringing the bride to the
huppah' – and was marked by the congregation processing to
the bride's home for the act of 'delivering the bride to the
bridegroom'. This took place in the morning before the actual
wedding ceremony amidst much rejoicing and hilarity. *B'deken*
marks the very beginning of *kiddushin* (the marriage ceremony). The couple is forbidden to others, the bride 'set aside'
for the groom and the groom for the bride. The veil symbolizes
the couple's separateness and, as has sometimes been suggested, other-worldliness.

The form of *b'deken* suggested here includes not only the
act of veiling the bride, but also a preliminary stage of the
marriage service for both bride and groom. The rabbi
addresses the couple, and then each member of their families
who are with them is invited to recite a verse from the Bible or
the liturgy in which the theme of holiness is used in seven different ways. Though the emphasis of marriage is on the
couple themselves and their act of consecration to each other,
they are nevertheless placed into a social and universal context.
In other words, they are not isolated from the world in which
they have been placed.

Stage-managing *b'deken* is not always easy. Once the bride
has arrived at the synagogue or the place of marriage, the
groom and the family who will stand underneath the *huppah*
with the couple should be shepherded to a quiet room or space
away from the congregation. Here the rabbi should explain
that this private moment marks the beginning of the wedding
service and blessings. This is a very intimate moment and can
be a quiet time of reflection and appreciation just before the

marriage itself. When Rebecca left her family in Haran to travel to Canaan to be married to Isaac, her mother and brother recited the words: 'Our sister, may you be the mother of thousands, of tens of thousands.' While this verse may not be appropriate for us today, this ceremony should still convey the concern and love of those close to the couple and help prepare them for the solemnity of the marriage blessings.

The rabbi says

In the quietness of this moment, before your marriage to each other, we pause to offer you our love and invoke God's blessing upon you both. Set the Eternal One always before you at your right hand, let God not be moved. May your hearts be glad and your souls rejoice as you set forth to be married to each other. May you be strengthened by your love for one another and supported by your family around you. In the trials and difficulties of life, may you protect each other and may your love become deeper and your trust in each other made more secure in the years ahead. May you know God's ways and walk in God's paths, protected by God's tender mercy.

Members of the family each say

1. Consecrate your lives to each other and be holy, as it is written: 'You shall be holy, for I the Eternal One your God am holy' (Leviticus 19.1).

2. O God, in your goodness you renew the work of creation day by day. May the earth rejoice in your marriage, as it is written: 'Holy, holy, holy is the Eternal One of all creation, the whole earth is full of your glory' (Isaiah 6.3).

3. 'Guardian of a holy people, preserve the remnant of a holy people; let not a holy people perish, who repeat the threefold sanctification to the Holy One' (from the liturgy).

4. 'You chose us from among all peoples; you loved and

favoured us and exalted us above all tongues and sanctified us by your commandments' (from the liturgy).

5. 'I remember the devotion of your youth, your love as a bride, how you followed me in the wilderness in a land not sown. Israel was holy to the Eternal One, the first fruits of God's harvest' (Jeremiah 2.2–3).

6. Be constant and faithful to each other, sanctify yourselves in each other's eyes, as it is written: 'Keep my statutes and observe them; I am the Eternal One, I sanctify you' (Leviticus 20.1), and further on: 'Set me as a seal upon your heart, as a seal upon your arm . . . Many waters cannot quench love, neither can floods drown it' (Song of Songs 6–7).

7. 'Sing to the Eternal One, sing praises, tell of God's wonderful works. Glory in God's holy name; let the hearts of those who seek the Eternal One rejoice. Seek the Eternal One and God's strength, seek God's presence continually' (based on I Chronicles 16.9–11). Let those who walk down to the *huppah* praise your name, O God, entering into this covenant of love and truth, of faithfulness and peace.

The couple say to each other

I betroth you to me for ever.	וְאֵרַשְׂתִּיךְ לִי לְעוֹלָם
I betroth you to me with integrity and justice, with tenderness and love.	וְאֵרַשְׂתִּיךְ לִי בְּצֶדֶק וּבְמִשְׁפָּט וּבְחֶסֶד וּבְרַחֲמִים:
I betroth you to me with faithfulness, and you shall know the Eternal One.	וְאֵרַשְׂתִּיךְ לִי בֶּאֱמוּנָה וְיָדַעַתְּ אֶת־יְהֹוָה:

The groom and unterfuehren *make their way to the huppah.*

The bride and her attendants follow.

'Marriage' by Any Other Name: Lesbian and Gay 'Commitment Ceremonies'

Elizabeth Tikvah Sarah

The politics of language: what we call 'it'

What are lesbian and gay 'commitment ceremonies'? In recent years, this appellation has entered into public discourse to describe a new phenomenon in the lives of lesbian and gay people: the public declaration of a couple's commitment to one another in the form of a ceremony or ritual – hence the name.

But the term 'commitment ceremonies' begs a host of questions. How do commitment ceremonies differ from heterosexual marriage? Do the differences between them revolve around the sexuality and gender of those concerned or are they about matters of content – or both? To what extent does our understanding of the term 'commitment ceremonies' depend on who is using it? What difference does it make if the term is chosen by a couple to encapsulate the bond they are making with one another, or is promoted by commentators in an effort to interpret a social phenomenon outside their experience? What are the political and the religious implications of labelling the contracts that lesbian and gay couples are entering into as commitment ceremonies rather than marriage?

It is self-evident (to me, at least) that the bonds which some lesbian and gay couples are choosing to make with one another are both like and *unlike* the bonds which heterosexual couples make with one another. On the one hand, in both cases, couples are making a public declaration of a covenant between them. On the other hand, only in the case of heterosexual couples is this covenant recognized by the state as legally binding and regarded by the traditions of all the major religions as divinely ordained.

Whatever difference differing sexualities may make to the experience and understanding of sharing a covenant on the part of couples themselves, the distinction currently being made in the arena of public discourse between heterosexual marriages and lesbian and gay commitment ceremonies reflects the historic presumption that heterosexual unions alone are valid. The most important aspect of the development of 'commitment ceremonies' is that after millennia lesbian and gay couples are challenging this presumption.

What is marriage?

Heterosexual marriage is an historical institution. It has changed over time. The label may have remained constant since days of old, but 'marriage' is not the same phenomenon today that it was. In addition, the meaning and the content of 'marriage' varies according to its particular religious/cultural/ethnic/geographical/economic/political setting. The evidence from the Bible suggests that Jewish marriage began in the form of the acquisition of a young virgin by a man from her father (see Deuteronomy 22.13–28). As the early rabbinic sages examined the legal texts of the Bible over two thousand years ago, they brought these together with the theological perspective of the biblical Creation narratives (Genesis 1 and 2) and the romantic-love lyricism of the biblical book, The Song of Songs, in their task of creating the rules and rituals of Jewish marriage (see the Babylonian Talmud tractate, *Kiddushin*, edited c. 500 CE). These rules and rituals remain largely in force throughout the Jewish world to this day – with some 'progressive' adjustments – in the face of massive social transformations.

So, Jewish marriage retains an element of acquisition of the bride by the groom, known as *kinyan*, an element of reciprocal covenantal love, and an underlying theology of God's dual purpose in creating humanity in two forms, male and female: the imperative of reproduction on the one hand (Genesis 1.27–28) and the need for companionship on the other (Genesis 2.18–25).

Originally two ceremonies separated in time – one involving betrothal (*Erusin* – also known as *Kiddushin*) and one, the marriage itself (*Nissu'in*) – the wedding ritual is conducted in two parts within one ceremony. In the first part, the dimension of acquisition is expressed by the groom placing a ring on the bride's index finger and saying the the words of a legal formula of betrothal: 'You are betrothed to me by this ring according to the law of Moses and Israel.' And the notion of marriage as an economic arrangement is underlined in the words of the traditional contract document (the *k'tubah*), signed by two witnesses before the ceremony, which sets out the husband's financial obligations towards his wife. In the second part of the ceremony, the theme of covenant is expressed, together with the Divine purpose underlying heterosexual union, in the recitation of Seven Blessings (*Sheva B'rakhot*) which celebrate the groom and the bride.

Since the understanding of marriage as a loving partnership has become predominant in Western societies during the second half of the twentieth century, progressive Jewish movements have altered the traditional ritual and procedures of marriage ceremonies to reflect this, making the formula of betrothal reciprocal, supporting couples in their wish to exchange rings, and re-writing the *k'tubah* so that it has become a document which expresses the couple's promises to love and support one another. In making these changes, Progressive Judaism has succeeded in completely undercutting the original aspect of *kinyan*, acquisition of the bride by the groom, while preserving the outward forms.

The best-known symbol of a Jewish wedding, the canopy (*huppah*) under which the bride and groom stand, provides the most dramatic expression of the change in the meaning of Jewish marriage from biblical times to the present day. Originally, there was no ceremony attached to the acquisition of a bride by a groom – he would simply take her into his home and have sex with her. The 'memory' of this form of marriage is present in the *huppah*, and the canopy has also accumulated meanings so that today it also represents the quality of the home that the couple hope to create together.

Aping heterosexual marriage?

Marriage is a changing phenomenon, and while many ritual elements appear to be the same, their meanings have changed. However, marriage was and has remained to this day an institution for regulating heterosexual unions. So what has it got to do with lesbian and gay people? From a Jewish perspective, the institution of marriage emerged in a context in which there was no concept of same-sex relationships. The Bible's condemnation of two men 'lying' with one another (Leviticus 18.22; 20.13) centres on a prohibition against sex between men – and there is no mention of two women lying together, because throughout the biblical treatment of sex, with the exception of bestiality, it is men alone who act and initiate. The focus of the Bible's concern is with prohibiting sexual acts associated with the practices of other peoples (specifically, those of Canaan and Egypt, Leviticus 18.3).

And yet, when the rabbis commented on the verses in Leviticus 18 and 20 (in a work of halakhic midrash – legal exegesis of the Torah – edited at the end of the fourth century), they not only brought the notion of sex between women into the picture, but they explained that the people Israel were prohibited from following the 'laws' of Egypt and Canaan because in those societies 'a man would marry (*nosei*) a man and a woman would marry a woman' (*Sifra, Acharei Mot* 9.8. For a discussion of Jewish law on homosexuality see Sarah, 1995; Mariner, 1995).

The ongoing reality of same-sex relationships and marriages constitutes the 'underside' of the chronicle of humanity, a largely unwritten history. It has only been in the last three decades of the twentieth century that lesbian and gay life has become more visible – in the Western world at least. And as same-sex relationships have emerged from the shadows, so increasing numbers of lesbian and gay couples today are choosing to lay claim to the public recognition of their commitment to one another, are choosing to celebrate their relationships and 'marry' one another (see Balka and Rose, 1989; Berner and Primack, 1994; Butler, 1990; Gilbert, 1996; Elwell, 1998; Martinac, 1998; Sherman, 1992; Smith and Saxe, 1991). Whatever term a couple may decide to call the bond they are forging between them, if we weren't talking about same-gender relationships, the obvious label to use would be 'marriage'. Heterosexuals know this and so do lesbian and gay people. That is why there is considerable opposition to it – on both sides. For heterosexual critics, 'marriage' is their exclusive prerogative, an eternal sign of the special status of heterosexual relationships; for lesbian and gay critics, it is precisely because 'marriage' is a heterosexual institution that lesbian and gay people should have nothing to do with it and should continue to live differently.

The critics on both sides share the fear that lesbian and gay unions will erode the difference between heterosexuality and homosexuality and promote the notion that 'we are all the same'. This fear echoes that expressed by the opponents of women's liberation in the 1970s, that if women and men ceased to play different roles, we would all become androgynous. The evidence of the past twenty-five years indicates both that the struggle for equality continues and that when women and men are ostensibly doing the same things, they don't end up being the same. The biological/psychological/ sociological reality of what it is to be born and to be socialized as a female or a male persists and women and men continue to express their differing experience of life when they are engaged in the same tasks.

We are all the same – we are all different. When lesbian and gay couples get 'married' they don't stop being lesbians and gay men. Lesbians and gay men are re-defining 'marriage' for themselves, making it in their own image. And when they do this, they are actually part of a much broader phenomenon. One of the consequences of the transformation of gender roles in the last quarter of the twentieth century is that heterosexual marriages have been changing. In fact, in a sense, the differences between heterosexual marriages today and those which pre-date feminism are as great as the differences which differentiate heterosexual unions from homosexual ones. Indeed, the differences have become so immense that one could argue that many heterosexual 'marriages' today no longer 'fit' neatly into the concept of marriage promulgated by religious institutions and the state. What is more, marriage is not only changing, it is becoming much less prevalent. In a climate in which fewer and fewer heterosexuals are getting 'married', the notion of 'marriage' as a choice defined by those who choose it, rather than as an inevitable state of existence for all heterosexual adults, is becoming more and more significant. And it is in this climate that we have witnessed the emergence of lesbian and gay marriage.

Every year, fewer and fewer marriages take place. However, a sizable proportion of heterosexual people are choosing to get married, and increasing numbers of lesbian and gay couples are choosing likewise. In a society in which cohabitation is no longer considered 'living in sin' and the life-style choices for adults are many and varied, why do many people still want to get married? There are as many answers to this question as there are couples getting married.

Re-defining Kiddushin

The traditional Jewish rationale for *Kiddushin* as the exclusive prerogative of heterosexual couples is rooted in the understanding that humanity was made in two forms, male and female, in order that these two forms might re-unite for the purposes of reproduction and companionship. This bi-polar reading which focusses on the anatomical distinction between the sexes as delineated in the first Creation story, where the words male (*zahar*) and female (*n'keivah*) are used (Genesis 1.27), ignores the implications of the fact that both male and female are created as two aspects of a singular human being (*Adam*) 'in the image of God' (1.27), and that in the second creation story the similarity between the two sexes is underlined with the use of the words woman, *ishah*, and man, *ish*, both of which derive from the same root, *alef, nun, shin*, to be *human* (2.23) (Sarah, 1992).

While the Jewish concept of holiness, *k'dushah*, is bound up with the notion of making separations, and this is reflected in the betrothal ritual (*Erusin – Kiddushin*), in which the bride is set apart for the groom, the marriage service as a whole is actually quite paradoxical. While the bride is consecrated to the groom in the first section of the ceremony in which the *difference* between them is emphasized, they are joined together in the *singular* image of humanity (*Adam*) in Eden in the Seven Blessings (*Sheva B'rakhot*), which are recited in the second section of the ceremony.

Humanity is one. Humanity is also differentiated. While the Creation narratives posit differentiation simply in bi-polar terms, it is becoming increasingly evident that the differences within humanity are much more complex. Same-sex couples may share the same gender, but may express that gender differently, and indeed, be different from one another in a host of ways. Heterosexual couples may be divided by the outward 'signs' of gender, but share a similar disposition and way of being in the world. A ceremony that acknowledges the ways in which the individuals concerned are different from one another ritualizes their consecration to one another, and celebrates their union, is equally relevant for all couples. A ceremony that includes these elements is *Kiddushin*.

As I have argued elsewhere, 'the Jewish concept of holiness

sets apart and embraces different elements' (Sarah, 1996, 72). Just as it is possible to work out a 'new Jewish sexual ethic' that is inclusive, that applies equally to all sexual relationships between adults (ibid.), so it is also possible, with a little imagination, to re-define *Kiddushin* in such a way that includes the sanctification and celebration of same-sex unions. The reality is that many lesbian and gay couples are choosing to formalize and celebrate their commitment to one another. The time has come for the religious institutions and the state to acknowledge this reality positively by expanding their understandings of 'marriage' to embrace same-sex relationships.

References

Balka, Christie and Andy Rose, 1989. *Twice Blessed. On Being Lesbian, Gay and Jewish*, Beacon Press

Berner, Leila Gal and Renee Gal Primack, 1994. 'Lesbian Commitment Ceremonies', in Debra Orenstein (ed.), *Life Cycles. Jewish Women on Life Passages and Personal Milestones*, Jewish Lights Publishing

Butler, Becky, 1990. *Ceremonies of the Heart. Celebrating Lesbian Unions*, Seal Press

Elwell, Sue Levi, 1998. 'Honor the Holiness of Lesbian and Gay Marriages', *Reform Judaism*, Winter

Gilbert, Beth, 1996. 'Gays and Lesbians under the Chuppah', *Reform Judaism*, Summer

Johnson, Susan E., 1990. *Long Term Lesbian Couples*, Naiad Press

—, 1995. *For Love and Life. Intimate Portraits of Lesbian Couples*, Naiad Press

Mariner, Rodney, 1995. 'The Jewish Homosexual and the Halachic Tradition', in Jonathan Magonet (ed.), *Jewish Explorations of Sexuality*, Berghaan Books

Martinac, Paula, 1998. *The Lesbian and Gay Book of Love and Marriage*, Broadway Books

Sarah, Elizabeth, 1992. 'The Biblical Account of the First Woman: A Jewish Feminist Perspective', in Teresa Elwes (ed.), *Women's Voices. Essays in Contemporary Feminist Theology*, HarperCollins

—, 1995. 'Judaism and Lesbianism: A Tale of Life on the Margins of the Text', in Jonathan Magonet (ed.), *Jewish Explorations of Sexuality*, Berghaan Books

—, 1996. 'Towards a New Jewish Sexual Ethic', in Jonathan A. Romain (ed.), *Renewing the Vision. Rabbis Speak Out on Modern Jewish*

Issues, SCM Press

Sherman, Suzanne, 1992. *Lesbian and Gay Marriages*, Temple University Press

Smith, Moon and Susan Saxe, 1991. 'A Commitment Celebration', in Elizabeth Resnick Levine (ed.), A *Ceremonies Sampler. New Rites, Celebrations and Observances of Jewish Women*, San Diego, CA, Woman's Institute for Continuing Jewish Education, San Diego, CA

Our Jewish Wedding

Elizabeth Tikvah Sarah

The power of symbols

As Jewish lesbians claiming Jewish marriage for ourselves, my partner and I hoped to demonstrate that when two women get married it both is and isn't like any other wedding, and that talking about the 'marriage' of two women is as appropriate as calling any covenantal union between two lovers and companions 'marriage' at the end of the twentieth century.

In the 'Introduction' to the service we prepared for our wedding, which took place on 14 June 1998, Cathy and I wrote:

> This ceremony celebrates our commitment to one another and to the traditions, both Jewish and lesbian, which are central to our lives.
>
> We have called it a Covenant of Love, *B'rit Ahavah*, for two reasons: because the theme of covenant is so crucial to Judaism in general and to the traditional Jewish marriage service in particular; and because the notion of two individuals establishing a committed relationship rooted in equality, mutuality and reciprocity is fundamental to the values of lesbian existence and community.
>
> The traditional name for Jewish marriage, *Kiddushin*, expresses the idea that the couple are separated from the 'forbidden' relationships proscribed in the Torah (Leviticus 18 and 20) and consecrated to one another. In the traditional ceremony, although the loving covenant between the couple is celebrated, the bride is 'acquired' by the groom. Since we neither accept the notion that same-sex relationships are 'forbidden', nor the concept of ownership, our

ceremony is not *Kiddushin* in the technical sense. However, our ceremony includes elements which acknowledge that from this day onwards we are consecrated to one another, and find inspiration in Jewish understandings of 'holiness' which define 'holy' living as the pursuit of justice and the creation of loving, respectful relationships between people.

So, our ceremony is both like and unlike a traditional Jewish wedding! It both is and is not *Kiddushin*. The framework is identical, the content is quite similar in places, but the emphasis it places on equality, mutuality and reciprocity make it radically different.

Cathy and I wanted to get married and we wanted to get married Jewishly. At the same time, our understanding of our Jewish wedding was informed by the tradition of lesbian unions (Faderman, 1985; Johnson 1990; 1995), the values of lesbian community, and our experience as lesbians. In working out the content of our wedding and thinking through the structure and rituals of the traditional marriage ceremony, the meaning of our lives as lesbians was as important to us as our understanding of our lives as Jews. The consciousness and experience of both as they merge together in us as individuals and in our relationship were the living waters out of which we created our ceremony. The end-result of this process looked very Jewish, while being very lesbian at the same time. And most important, it reflected who we are and what we mean to each other completely. And that's the paradox – and the challenge: the future of marriage as an enduring institution is contingent upon couples choosing it and making it their own.

Our Jewish wedding

Cathy and I took many of the key symbols, elements and rituals of a traditional Jewish wedding and re-invented them for ourselves. This is what we chose to do with our ceremony. The material available to date of Jewish lesbian and gay marriages (see, for example, Smith and Saxe, 1991 – and the testimonies included in Balka and Rose, 1989; Butler, 1990; Martinac, 1998; Sherman, 1992) suggests that there is a wide variety of approaches and forms, and that while some couples choose to use the words 'wedding' and 'marriage', others prefer, for example, 'commitment ceremony', 'covenant of love', 'covenant of lovers'. Because we began with the understanding that what we were doing was both like and unlike a traditional wedding, we choose both to call it a *B'rit Ahavah*, 'Covenant of Love', to emphasize its difference, and to express it in the language and ritual of Jewish marriage to demonstrate that what is the same can be completely different, too.

Our marriage ritual began with the signing of a document, *k'tubah*, which we had written ourselves, drawing on biblical materials and ideas from the *k'tubot* of lesbian and gay couples who had trod the way before us distributed on the Internet under the heading *Sample k'tubah Texts*. In writing the *k'tubah* we were assisted by two rabbinic colleagues – both men – one gay, the other heterosexual. For us, the place of what we were doing within the Jewish community, whether or not the majority within that community recognized it, was facilitated by the participation of Jewish friends and allies. Our *k'tubah* expresses our promises to one another and, critically for us, acknowledges each one of us as individuals, pledging to ensure that we continue to nourish ourselves as well as one another. Our *k'tubah* includes a declaration of the new shared middle name we have taken, *Tikvah*, meaning 'hope'. That name not only expresses a value that is central to our lives; its place as a shared middle name proclaims both our new shared identity and the continuation of our separate identities. We were inspired to take a shared middle name by the example of American Reconstructionist rabbi, Leila Gal Berner, and her partner, Renee Gal Primack (1994).

The witnesses to our *k'tubah* were close long-term lesbian friends. After our *k'tubah* was signed by them and also by our officiating rabbi, Barbara Borts – a close heterosexual woman friend – and by ourselves, Cathy and I spent a few minutes alone together. The traditional wedding includes a ritual called *b'deken*, when the groom, in memory of Jacob's experience of finding himself married to Leah rather than Rachel (Genesis 29.23–25), goes into the room where his bride is secluded, and either lifts her veil or covers her face with the veil to check that she is who he expects her to be. For us, the asymmetry and sexism which provides the rationale for the ritual was alien to our experience. In place of a one-sided 'unveiling' we looked into each other's eyes and checked each other out. Before we embarked on the journey to the *huppah* which would change our lives, we wanted to face each other and acknowledge what we were doing.

We were each accompanied on that journey. Traditionally, the groom waits under the *huppah* and the bride is escorted by her female relatives – in more recent years, under the influence of mainstream culture, by her father. Cathy walked first, supported on one side by a close friend, on the other by her sister. I followed, supported also by a close friend and by my sister. For both of us, our connections to our families is very important, and the family members who attended were those who accept and celebrate our relationship.

The 'order' of our walk down the aisle was quite deliberate. We wanted to make the point that although I have a professional relationship to Judaism, and have, indeed, conducted many weddings myself, I was walking down the aisle as an individual, not a rabbi. In addition to that reason, I had already had a wedding – twenty-three years earlier, I had been heterosexually married. This was a 'first' for Cathy, and so it was appropriate that she should go first. And we maintained that order throughout the ceremony. As we walked down the aisle, we were followed by two 'bridesmaids' – my sister's daughters of seven and five respectively – who had chosen their own 'fairy' dresses, complete with wings, and insisted on being called 'bridesmaids' and dressing appropriately, even if their aunts were rather unusual 'brides'! For those who are curious to know our attire, we both wore silk trouser suits: mine was cream 'raw' silk in a round-collared 'Indian' style; Cathy's was more tailored and a sea blue/green colour. In choosing our clothes, we weren't interested in making any 'ideological' statements; we each wore what suits us best.

The *huppah* consisted of four wooden poles which we had purchased from a timber merchant and the large white *tallit I* wear during the Days of Awe each year. We had covered the poles with white ribbon and decorated the tops of each one with flowing streams of silver ribbon. Our *huppah* was a combination of simplicity, solemnity, joy and fun. We wanted to signal that while what we were doing was very serious, it was also party-time. Each pole was held by a close friend.

As in a traditional wedding, our *huppah* represented the home we were making together, open on all sides as a sign of our hospitality and an acknowledgment that our home was part of a community and that our relationship exists in the context of a network of relationships. In addition to the four pole-holders, sisters, friends, and the rabbi, in the second half of the ceremony a series of different people came under the chuppah, to recite one of the seven blessings – friends old and young, single and coupled, able-bodied and disabled, women and men, homosexual and heterosexual – all welcome in our home. Of course, we didn't choose people because they fitted a particular 'category'. The reality is that the life we share as a couple and our lives as individuals are peopled by different people. And that variety was also reflected in the one hundred other guests who celebrated with us.

As we walked down the aisle, our rabbi led the congregation in singing Psalm 150, the 'Halleluyah' Psalm – one of our favourites. Heart-thumping and ecstatic, that psalm expressed our joy, our desire to sing and dance and praise the One who created and sustains life:

Halleluyah! Praise God in the sanctuary.
Praise God whose power the heavens proclaim.
Praise God's mighty deeds.
Praise God's abundant greatness.
Praise God with shofar blast.
Praise God with lyre and harp.

Praise God with timbrel and dance.
Praise God with lute and pipe.
Praise God with cymbals sounding.
Praise God with cymbals resounding.
Let every soul praise the Eternal One. Halleluyah!

Once we arrived under the *huppah*, we stood side by side,
choosing neither for one of us to circle the other seven times –
traditionally the bride circles the groom – nor for us both to
circle each other. Having experienced our form of *b'deken* and
drawn the veil away from our souls, all we wanted to do now
was to begin.

As we stood under the *huppah*, the traditional welcome,
blessing 'those who come in the name of Adonai', couched in
the masculine form, was reformulated in the words of the
American Jewish singer/song-writer, Debbie Friedman, in both
feminine and masculine plural form:

Blessed are those who come under the wings of the
Sh'khinah.
May you be blessed beneath the wings of the *Sh'khinah*,
be blessed with love, be blessed with peace.

We wanted a welcome that included everyone present and
spoke of God as a sheltering presence. For this reason, we did
not include the declaration which traditionally follows the
welcome, *Mi Adir*, which speaks of God being 'supreme' and
'blessed above all'. While acknowledging God's power as the
Source of Life and the Spirit that infuses the Universe, the
image of God as a mighty Sovereign ruling over us is not part
of our experience of God.

In place of *Mi Adir*, we included a prayer, slightly re-worked
from one offered in the Marriage Service of the Reform
Synagogues of Great Britain, asking for God's blessing on our
life together. This prayer closed with the words of the blessing
Jews say when something 'new' is happening. In our translation of this blessing, we addressed God as Sovereign-Presence

of the Universe, rather than Sovereign or King of the Universe. This subtle change, used in our translation of all the blessings of the service, expresses our understanding of God as a power within the universe rather than a power over it:

> Our Living God, we stand before Your holiness, and in quietness thank you for bringing us to this time. May Your love protect Cathy and Elli who ask you to bless them. They ask Your blessing not for themselves alone but for each other, and for their life together, for in Your blessing is loyalty and devotion, love and trust. Be with them, Eternal One, so that they may know true happiness and bring joy to all who love them. Let them honour You and so bring honour to themselves.
>
> Blessed are You, Our Living God, Sovereign-Presence of the Universe, Who has kept us alive and supported us and brought us to this time.

Perhaps the biggest challenge of the traditional ceremony is the part dealing with the 'betrothal'. 'Betrothal' is traditionally understood in the context of the acquisition of the bride by the groom, reflected in the traditional blessing of betrothal and in the groom's declaration. Having looked at various texts distributed on the Internet under the title *Kiddushin Ceremonies for Lesbian and Gay Couples*, we realized that all the alternative formulations, both lesbian/gay and progressive, failed to tackle the traditional understanding of *Kiddushin* as the act of consecrating the bride to the groom, but not vice versa.

The notion of *Kiddushin* as the setting apart of the bride for the groom derives from the biblical meaning of holiness, *k'dushah*, which is concerned with separating Israel from the nations. However, even within its biblical setting, *k'dushah* goes beyond mere 'separation' to a notion of holy living that embraces the pursuit of justice and the creation of loving, respectful relationships between people (see the 'Holiness Code', Leviticus 19). Because the notion of Covenant was our central theme, coupled with an understanding of *k'dushah* as holy living in its broadest sense, we felt it was essential that the blessing of betrothal which introduced our declarations to one another should be in keeping with our sense of our relationship as a loving partnership formed in the presence of God who sanctifies our lives. And so we wrote our own text (in Hebrew and English). As in a traditional wedding, the blessing was preceded by a blessing of the 'fruit of the wine', with which Jews celebrate all holy occasions:

> Blessed are You, Our Living God, Sovereign-Presence of the Universe, who creates the fruit of the vine.
>
> Our Living God, Who remembers the covenant and Who has made us holy through Your commandments, these loving companions stand before You ready to enter into a sacred Covenant of Love. Blessed are You, Eternal One, Who dwells in our midst and sanctifies our lives.

The betrothal formulation with which we each, in turn, placed a ring on the finger of our betrothed, began in the traditional way, but ended very differently. By definition, it is not possible for a bride to acquire a bride! And anyway, clearly our ceremony was not 'according to the law of Moses and Israel'. Instead, we felt that it was 'in the spirit of the people and the traditions of Israel' – a spirit which celebrates love and life, traditions which are manifold and which come to life every time Jews express the meaning of their lives through the medium of Jewish language and symbols:

> By this ring you are consecrated to me in the spirit of the people and the traditions of Israel.

Following this declaration, we proclaimed our promises to one another and our hopes for our relationship – all of which are included in our *k'tubah*. We proclaimed our promises in turn and then, together, expressed our hopes:

In turn:

I betroth you to me for ever, I betroth you to me with integrity and justice, with tenderness and love. I betroth you to me with faithfulness (Hosea 2.21–22).

I will cherish you, honour you and support you. I will share in your joys and in your sorrows. I will respect you and the Divine image within you.

Wherever you will go, I will go, and wherever you will lodge, I will lodge; your people shall be my people and your God my God (Ruth 1.16).

Together:

May our life together nourish, enrich and challenge us as individuals and connect us ever more closely to the communities in which we live.

May our home be filled with love and learning, generosity and celebration and be a source of blessing to all who enter.

The Hebrew language knows no neutral forms – everything is either 'feminine' or 'masculine'. The declaration of betrothal, because it is traditionally said by a groom to his bride, is of course in the feminine form. The text we took from the prophet Hosea, declaring the betrothal of God to Israel, is also in the feminine form because, traditionally, God is Israel's groom. And, of course, the words of Ruth to Naomi are those of one woman to another. So we were able to use these passages as they were without alteration. However, the Hebrew rendering of the promises and hopes which we wrote ourselves proved quite difficult. And we only accomplished the task of expressing contemporary concepts in an ancient language with the assistance of one of my colleagues.

The betrothal part of our ceremony completed, we were addressed by our rabbi who reflected on the personal and the 'political' dimensions of our wedding.

The second part of the proceedings opened with the reading of the *k'tubah* in English and Hebrew by Rabbi Mark Solomon.

After the *k'tubah* reading, the celebration of our covenant with the recitation of the *Sheva B'rakhot* (Seven Blessings) represented perhaps the most traditional dimension of our wedding. Apart from changing 'bride' and 'groom' to 'lovers' and 'loving companions' in the Hebrew and the English, and writing an inclusive translation, we decided to keep most of the words of the traditional text for three main reasons. First, because this was the section of the traditional ceremony which celebrated the partnership aspect of Jewish marriage that was central to our understanding. Second, because it is precisely within the *Sheva B'rakhot* that the image of Creation is invoked as the theological underpinning for heterosexual marriage, and we wanted to assert our claim to being part of humanity, creatures of God. Not because we subscribe to the notion that we were 'born' lesbians. Sexuality is a complex matter. Although we are all born with the potential to be 'sexual', it is not clear how anyone comes to express a particular form of sexuality. The issue for us is that we are lesbians who like all human beings were created in the image of God. The third reason for retaining the text of the *Sheva B'rakhot* with only slight emendations was because we wanted to hear the blessings sung for us, to hear our union celebrated in the same way that heterosexual unions are celebrated. For this reason, after a series of friends came under the *huppah* to recite each blessing in turn, our rabbi sang them:

Blessed are You, our Living God, Sovereign-Presence of the Universe, Who creates the fruit of the vine.

Blessed are You, our Living God, Sovereign-Presence of the Universe, Who created all things for Your glory.

Blessed are You, our Living God, Sovereign-Presence of the Universe, Creator of Humankind.

Blessed are You, our Living God, Sovereign-Presence of the Universe, Who created humankind in Your image and in Your likeness. Blessed are You, Eternal One, Creator of Humankind.

May lonely Zion rejoice as her children are returned to her

in joy. Blessed are You, Eternal One, Who causes Zion to rejoice with her children.

May these lovers and companions rejoice as did Your first creatures in Eden long ago. Blessed are You, Eternal One, Who causes these loving companions to rejoice.

Blessed are You, our Living God, Sovereign-Presence of the Universe, Who created happiness and joy, exultation, song, pleasure, delight, love, harmony, peace and companionship. Soon, our Living God, may there be heard in the cities of Judah and in the courtyards of Jerusalem, the sounds of happiness and the sounds of joy, the sounds of lovers' jubilation from their *huppah*. Blessed are You, Eternal One, Who causes these loving companions to rejoice.

By making the words of the *Sheva B'rakhot* speak for our relationship as two women, we challenged the central presumption of the exclusive heterosexual claim to marriage, that heterosexual unions alone are 'natural' and part of God's Creation. We decided to retain the phrases related to Zion and Jerusalem because for us, as for many Jews, these places are bound up with the hopes for the future expressed by the Jewish prophets of old, when Jerusalem will live up to its Hebrew name, *Yerushalayim*, 'city of peace', and war will cease for ever.

The powerful symbol of Jerusalem as a sign of hope in the future is matched in the traditional wedding by the breaking of glass in remembrance of the destruction of the city at times in our history when all hope seemed lost. From a Jewish perspective, joy and sorrow are both integral to life, so even at a time of great joy – in the midst of a wedding – we acknowledge grief and pain. For Cathy and me, it was important to make a connection with our own sorrows, and for us each to break a glass to mark our own personal losses. But before we moved on to this final act of the ceremony, which also forced us to remember the struggle we had gone through to reach the day of our wedding in the face of hostility and prejudice, we were honoured to receive the blessing of God invoked by Rabbi Lionel Blue, my tutor at Leo Baeck College and ordaining rabbi, a gay man whose life has been spent being *Godly and Gay* (1995). In invoking God's blessing, Lionel rendered the Hebrew of the traditional 'Priestly' formula in the feminine form, imaging God as *Sh'khinah*, the Presence who journeys with us in our lives.

So with the blessing of the *Sh'khinah* warming our hearts, we turned, finally, to the breaking of glass:

> Today, as Cathy and Elli each break a glass, each acknowledges the bundle of grief that she carries within her, even as her cup overflows.
>
> In particular, Elli, so recently made an orphan, bears the loss of her parents, Edie and Paul Klempner – both of whom would have 'danced' in their own ways at this wedding.
>
> In addition to their personal losses, Cathy and Elli grieve together for the intrusion of homophobia into their lives and pray that, as the glass shatters beneath their feet, so may the yoke of bigotry be broken *bimheirah b'yameinu* – speedily in our own days. Amen.

As with every wedding, the breaking glass broke the tension of the ceremony, and the whole congregation erupted into singing the traditional melody '*siman tov u'mazal tov*', 'a good sign and good luck', which soon became a musical extravaganza as the *klezmer* band we had booked entered and took up the tune.

Straight after the ceremony we secluded ourselves together for a brief few moments. Traditionally, *yichud* is the time when the marriage is consummated. For us it was a moment to be alone together in the midst of the communal celebration, hold one another, and say, 'we did it!'

References

Balka, Christie and Andy Rose, 1989. *Twice Blessed. On Being Lesbian, Gay and Jewish*, Beacon Press

Berner, Leila Gal and Renee Gal Primack, 1994. 'Lesbian Commitment

Ceremonies', in Debra Orenstein (ed.), *Life Cycles. Jewish Women on Life Passages and Personal Milestones*, Jewish Lights Publishing

Blue, Lionel. 1995. 'Godly and Gay', in Jonathan Magonet (ed.), *Jewish Explorations of Sexuality*, Berghaan Books

Butler, Becky, 1990. *Ceremonies of the Heart. Celebrating Lesbian Unions*, Seal Press

Faderman, Lillian, 1985. *Surpassing the Love of Men. Romantic Friendship and Love between Women from the Renaissance to the Present*, The Women's Press (first published by Morrow, New York 1981)

Johnson, Susan E., 1990. *Long Term Lesbian Couples*, Naiad Press

—, 1995. *For Love and Life. Intimate Portraits of Lesbian Couples*, Naiad Press

Martinac, Paula, 1998. *The Lesbian and Gay Book of Love and Marriage*, Broadway Books

Sherman, Suzanne, 1992. *Lesbian and Gay Marriages*, Temple University Press

Smith, Moon and Susan Saxe, 1991. 'A Commitment Celebration', in Elizabeth Resnick Levine (ed.), A *Ceremonies Sampler. New Rites, Celebrations and Observances of Jewish Women*, San Diego, CA: Woman's Institute for Continuing Jewish Education

On the Breakdown of
a Relationship

Helen Freeman

Our prayer book praises God who 'changes times and varies seasons . . . and makes day and night, rolling away the light before the darkness and the darkness before the light'.[1]

Jewish tradition acknowledges the place of God in all of human life and experience. There are in each individual life, as in the life of creation, light and darkness, times of great happiness and times of great grief.

Yet this reality conflicts with our expectations of life inculcated by a Western world that assumes that 'more' is always 'better' and that happiness is always attainable. We are brainwashed by a media that shows beautiful people with perfect hair and perfect teeth and perfect relationships. If by some unlucky chance those perfect relationships go wrong, then we are supposed to move seamlessly on to the next possibility, without looking back upon the failures and disappointments that we leave in our wake.

Those of us who have struggled through relationship breakdown and divorce know that, in the words of the song, 'it ain't necessarily so'. Relationship breakdown is one of the hardest things we have to cope with in life, particularly when the world is depicted as being full of happy couples. Gay or straight, long-term or short-term, any relationship breakdown is a site of broken dreams and lost hopes. It's a place of bereavement that needs careful handling, so that the bruised souls of the two individuals can be healed a little. Part of the healing process is to acknowledge the faults and unreal expectations on both sides, as well as to mourn the dreams that never came to fruition, before there can be closure on that part of the person's life.

Classically, Judaism has a ritual to mark the end of a marriage, the giving and receiving of a *get*. As one who received an Orthodox *get* following the breakdown of my first marriage, I can say with some feeling that the rabbis involved in the process try their best to be compassionate and make the ritual as meaningful as possible.

The traditional procedure is fraught with difficulties. It is unilateral, the *get* is given by the man to the woman, and she cannot initiate it in normal circumstances.

Worse still, there are men who choose to punish their ex-wife by refusing to issue a *get*, meaning that she is unable to remarry in a traditional synagogue and becomes an *agunah*, a woman chained to her ex-husband.

There are other people for whom the traditional rituals are not nearly broad enough in their application or accessibility. There are couples who want a more personal ritual to end their relationship, something that goes beyond the *halakhic* requirement to give and receive a *get*. Those Jews whose marriage to a non-Jew fails have no access to the rituals of their own tradition in order to mark the ending of their marriage. In modern times many partners never marry at all, and so they too have no access to the ritual of the *get*. Their avoidance of legal complications also disqualifies them from the symbolic ritual that expresses the emotions at such a painful time. The situation is more complex still for people in a gay relationship for whom legally recognized marriage is not an option.

What we all have in common is a reluctance to concentrate on something that feels like a failure, to face the feelings that come at the end of a relationship or a divorce.

However, since relationships begin with such high hopes, and sometimes with religious or secular rituals to contain them, a ritual to mark the end of that relationship can be very healing. Such a ritual needs to be carefully thought through, and acted out with the intention of transforming the person's inner or outer situation. It may be hugely satisfying to rip all his shirts to shreds or wipe all her precious files from the computer, but that is only in the short term! In the long term, a ritual should have a positive effect on the life of the person who instigated it, rather than offer them a chance to act out hostility at an ex-partner.

So the first thing to think of in devising such a ritual is to situate it in a supportive environment with supportive people. The choice must feel comfortable to that person: it might be in their own home, or in a beautiful place outdoors, or in the synagogue which already supplies a safe, holding environment.

Devising the ritual is very much a time for personal creativity. It has to fit the requirements for the person who has suffered the relationship breakdown or divorce. It shouldn't be too mystifying or intrusively 'religious', at least in a formal way. That being said, religious music, and the use of blessings or other texts in Hebrew, can be very powerful, because they have been containers for Jewish meaning over thousands of years.

The following ritual is only a suggestion, the bare bones of a framework which people can flesh out with their own experience and individual preferences.

The ritual

Have ready a bowl of beautiful stones – chosen as an appropriate symbol because Jewish people put them on a grave for remembrance – a jar or vase in which to keep them after the ceremony and another bowl for discarded stones. All participants enter and sit down in a circle in silence. It is helpful to have something calming and beautiful to concentrate on at the centre of the circle. It might be a scented candle or an arrangement of flowers or stones. After a short silence, the ritual is begun by introducing some meditative music; it might be a niggun, *which is gentle and repetitive, someone to play a musical instrument, or a tape of meaningful music.*

Reader
M'kor Hayyim,[2] Source of life and of blessing and of strength,
we come before you this day to ask for your help.

All read
We are Israel, descendants of the one who struggled with God
and with human beings and prevailed, so pain and struggle is
something knit into our very souls.

We are the descendants of the prophets and sages of Israel,
of Rabbi Akiva and Beruriah who knew great sadness, and yet
found the inner strength to integrate that struggle and so move
forward in their lives.

Reader
We knew the pain of the Jewish people in exile, who struggled
in impossible circumstances to honour Your name and to feel
the companionship of the *Sh'khinah*, the loving Presence, who
is with us wherever we go.

Yet sadness and loss is hard to bear, disappointment and
pain a great trial, so we ask Your help and blessing, for ......
whose relationship with ...... has broken down after ...... years

All sing
כָּל-הָעוֹלָם כֻּלּוֹ גֶּשֶׁר צַר מְאֹד, וְהָעִקָּר לֹא לְפַחֵד כְּלָל.
'Kol ha-olam kulo gesher tzar m'od, v'ha-ikkar lo l'fahed klal
All the world is a very narrow bridge, the essential thing is not
to be afraid.

Silent prayer and meditation
*The person marking the relationship breakdown or divorce is
asked to speak. (If they are too upset, they can prepare a text
beforehand which is given to a close friend or family member
to read during the ritual. Alternatively, they can have prepared
a document to read at this point that mirrors the* k'tubah.*)*

The person picks up a stone and says
I want to remember the good things we shared in our time together like laughter, hope, friendships and (*where appropriate*) children.
For each of the good things, they add one of the stones to the central position where the candle or flowers or stones are already situated.

The person takes up another stone and says
I want to let go of the bitterness and disappointment and despair that marked the end of our relationship.
For each of the bad things, one of the stones is put outside the circle enacting the ritual.

The bowl of stones is then passed around the circle so that others may add something good to the promises for the future by saying things like

I value my friendship with ...... and will be with her/him during the low times there might be.
For each of the promises of support, a stone is added to the central point so that there is a visible reminder that the person will not be alone in sadness, however low she or he might feel.

All present read
As those who came before us were blessed in the presence of the communities that sustained them, so we offer our blessings for one among us in need of healing.

......, may you have comfort and relief in the healing of body and mind, and may you return in time to health and wholeness and strength.[3]

The person marking the end of her or his relationship
Renew my vision, O God; give meaning to my life and substance to my hopes. Let me see that there can be no light and beauty without darkness and pain, so that I may grow beyond

this time of struggle and loss. Give me the courage to integrate all that I have learned in this time of confusion and disorientation, so that I can transform my life. Amen.

All sing
Im ein ani li, mi li,   אם אין אֲנִי לִי מִי לִי?
u-kh'she-ani l'atzmi mah ani,   וּכְשֶׁאֲנִי לְעַצְמִי מָה אֲנִי?
v'im lo akhshav eimatai.[4]   וְאִם לֹא עַכְשָׁיו אֵימָתַי?
If I am not for myself, who will be for me, and if I am only for myself, what am I, and if not now, when?

At the end of the ritual, the person takes the stones home to keep as a symbol of hope for the future.

The discarded stones can be buried in the ground with the support of a rabbi or friend and the following said.
As I return these stones to the earth from which they came, so I let go of the pain that was present in my relationship with ......
The cycle is complete and that time is over.

Ritual for Leaving, Arriving and Journeying

Marcia Plumb

Invite people to come and ask them to bring a gift of some kind that represents leaving, journeying or arrival. They will also be asked to give a blessing during the ritual.

All sit in a circle, a niggun *is sung.*

Reader
To every thing there is a season, and a time to every purpose under the heaven;
A time to give birth, and a time to die;
A time to plant, and a time to pluck up that which is planted;
A time to kill, and a time to heal;
A time to break down, and a time to build up;
A time to weep, and a time to laugh;
A time to mourn, and a time to dance;
A time to cast away stones, and a time to gather stones together;
A time to embrace, and a time to refrain from embracing;
A time to seek, and a time to lose;
A time to keep, and a time to cast away;
A time to rend, and a time to sew;
A time to keep silence, and a time to speak;
A time to love, and a time to hate;
A time of war, and a time of peace. (Ecclesiastes 3.1–8)

Reader

And the Eternal said to Abraham: Go for yourself, from your
land, from your birthplace, and from your family home to a
land that I will show you. And I will make you a great people
and I will bless you and make your name great and it will be a
blessing (Genesis 12.1–2).

*The leader recalls the leaving and arriving of our ancestors,
how they were blessed before they started, how they took
something with them, and how difficult the journey was and
how successful they were in the end.*

*Each person goes round the circle and speaks for one minute
in which she or he tells the story of a move they have made, be
it physical or emotional. As they tell their story, they put their
gift on a tray.*

*Then the circle becomes a tunnel with two lines of people,
with the one who is moving at the top of the passageway. The
mover goes in a figure-of-eight format from person to person.
As she faces each person, the person she faces will give her a
blessing, like peace of mind, health or contentment. Before
leaving each person, she will respond, 'I will take with me the
memory of ......' and mention something particular to that
person. She then moves on to the next person. At the end of the
passageway she discovers the tray of gifts – upon her arrival as
it were. The group goes after her and forms a circle again.*

All say

בָּרוּךְ אַתָּה יְיָ אֱלֹהֵינוּ מֶלֶךְ הָעוֹלָם שֶׁהֶחֱיָנוּ וְקִיְּמָנוּ וְהִגִּיעָנוּ לַזְּמַן הַזֶּה.

*Barukh ata Adonai, eloheinu melekh ha-olam, she-heheyanu,
v'kiyy'manu, v'higgi'anu la-z'man ha-zeh.*

Blessed are You God, Sovereign of the universe, who has kept
us alive, and sustained us, and brought us to this time.

All sing

L'khi lakh, to a land that I will show you
Leikh l'kha, to a place you do not know
L'khi lakh, on your journey I will bless you
And you shall be a blessing, you shall be a blessing

You shall be a blessing *l'khi lakh*.
L'khi lakh, and I shall make your name great
Leikh l'kha and all shall praise your name
L'khi lakh to the place that I will show you
L'simhat hayyim, L'simhat hayyim
L'simhat hayyim l'khi lakh.
You shall be a blessing, you shall be a blessing
You shall be a blessing *l'khi lakh*.

Debbie Friedman

In Pain and in Healing

Animal Kaddish

Hadassah Davis

Introduction

When I was seventeen my grandfather died. A long-standing family quarrel meant that I had only met him twice. The first time that I was introduced to him I was about ten. He was an overweight, red-faced, angry-looking man. He returned my gaze disinterestedly, reached into his pocket, handed me a coin, and waved me away. The second time I met him, my polite 'hello' was ignored. I went to his funeral and watched proceedings with curiosity – and growing anger.

Two years before, my dog, Tessa, had died. We'd had her since I was four. She was a constant source of love and delight. In an abusive childhood home, Tessa alone gave me uncritical affection. It was often Tessa that made returning home possible.

My father took her to the vet. She had cancer and would have to be put down. The date was arranged and I was told. I said goodbye to her in the morning, returned from school in the afternoon, and she was gone. One of the few good things in my childhood had been taken from me, without emotional preparation, without ceremony, without any recognition of what loss means.

So here I was, at my grandfather's funeral. Some of the adults were crying, most not. Everyone was dressed symbolically in black, a ceremonial service for a generally disliked man. Yet my loving, kind, affectionate Tessa had received nothing. Why?

Years later, I learned the 'reason'. Humans have souls and are therefore especially linked to their creator – God. Human

development has marked this special relationship with ceremonies, hence life-cycle events become determined by theology. A *b'rit milah* is the covenant. Marriage is a sanctification.
Theologically speaking, animals don't have souls, so no life-
cycle events mark their naming, their lives, or their deaths.

This has always left me uneasy. Who are we to determine
who has a soul? Surely that's God's province. Isn't allotting
souls only to ourselves just another example of human arro-
gance? Perhaps we are little more than fairly bright animals
ourselves.

Although arguing theology can be fun, ultimately I'm more
concerned about Judaism meeting people's raw, distressing,
hurting emotions. We have a psychologically solid method for
mourning – the funeral, *shiva*, *sh'loshim*, stone-setting and
annual *yahrzeit*. The bereaved person is moved along the
process, from intense distress in *shiva*, to beginning to take
faltering footsteps back into the world during *sh'loshim* and
the next several months. A final ceremony, the stone-setting,
marks the end of the mourning period. The annual *yahrzeit*
gives a time and space for remembrance.

Whether or not animals have a soul is profoundly irrelevant
for me. For an elderly person whose sole (as well as soul) companion is their pet, for a child whose misery is alleviated by
relationship to an animal, for a family for whom a pet is
another member of the family unit, its loss can be devastating,
painful and life detracting. A liturgy of mourning for the death
of a loved pet can only be helpful in moving someone along
what is essentially the same psychological process.

A year ago, one of our cats had to be put down suddenly one
Friday afternoon. We were bereft. We prepared our *Shabbat*
table as usual, but couldn't simply light the *Shabbat* candles as
if what we had experienced a few hours earlier was a mere
minor inconvenience. Instead, we held each other and cried.
We talked about Rambam, remembered all the pleasure he'd
given us, lit a *yahrzeit* candle and recited *kaddish*. Only after
we'd done this could we bring in *Shabbat*. The following week
we were helped in our grief and loss by friends and colleagues.

One particularly sensitive man wrote an enormously helpful letter of condolence. Their responses helped us feel that our feelings of devastation were legitimate and recognized. That week, I determined to try to write a pet bereavement liturgy.

I know there will be some who think this an utterly ridiculous idea. Well, there are many ridiculous ideas in the world and we all learn to live with them. Others, whose animals are a part of their hearts and lives, may find the following helpful.

Funeral service for a pet

And God spoke to Noah and to his children with him saying: I establish My covenant with you and your offspring to come, and with every living thing that is with you – birds, cattle, and every living thing on the earth with you, everything that comes out of the ark, every living thing on the earth.

וַיֹּאמֶר אֱלֹהִים אֶל־נֹחַ וְאֶל־בָּנָיו אִתּוֹ לֵאמֹר: וַאֲנִי הִנְנִי מֵקִים אֶת־בְּרִיתִי אִתְּכֶם וְאֶת־זַרְעֲכֶם אַחֲרֵיכֶם: וְאֵת כָּל־נֶפֶשׁ הַחַיָּה אֲשֶׁר אִתְּכֶם בָּעוֹף בַּבְּהֵמָה וּבְכָל־חַיַּת הָאָרֶץ אִתְּכֶם מִכֹּל יֹצְאֵי הַתֵּבָה לְכֹל חַיַּת הָאָרֶץ:

We patronize animals for their incompleteness, for their tragic fate of having taken form so far below ourselves. And therein we err, and greatly err. For the animal shall not be measured by us. In a world older and more complete than ours they move finished and complete, gifted with extensions of the senses we have lost or never attained, living by voices we shall never hear.

And God said: '. . . I shall remember My covenant between Me and you and every living thing of flesh . . .'

וַיֹּאמֶר אֱלֹהִים . . . וְזָכַרְתִּי אֶת־בְּרִיתִי אֲשֶׁר בֵּינִי וּבֵינֵיכֶם וּבֵין כָּל־נֶפֶשׁ חַיָּה בְּכָל בָּשָׂר . . .

We need another and wiser and perhaps more mystical concept of animals . . . They are not brethren, they are not underlings, they are other nations, caught with ourselves in the net of life and time, fellow prisoners of the splendour and travail of the earth.

Who sends forth springs into the valleys	הַמְשַׁלֵּחַ מַעְיָנִים בַּנְּחָלִים
Between the mountains they run;	בֵּין הָרִים יְהַלֵּכוּן:
They give drink to every animal of the field	יַשְׁקוּ כָּל־חַיְתוֹ שָׂדָי
The wild asses quench their thirst.	יִשְׁבְּרוּ פְרָאִים צְמָאָם:
Beside them dwell the birds of heaven,	עֲלֵיהֶם עוֹף־הַשָּׁמַיִם יִשְׁכּוֹן
From among the branches they sing.	מִבֵּין עֳפָאִים יִתְּנוּ־קוֹל:
Who waters the mountains from on high,	מַשְׁקֶה הָרִים מֵעֲלִיּוֹתָיו
The earth is full of the fruit of Your works.	מִפְּרִי מַעֲשֶׂיךָ תִּשְׂבַּע הָאָרֶץ:

God, full of compassion, exalted God, God of forgiveness, gracious and merciful, abundantly patient and full of love, grant perfect rest under the wings of Your presence, to the soul of .... who has gone to his/her eternal home. May he/she rest in peace. Amen.

אֵל מָלֵא רַחֲמִים שׁוֹכֵן בַּמְּרוֹמִים אֵלֶּה
סְלִיחוֹת חַנּוּן וְרַחוּם אֶרֶךְ אַפַּיִם וְרַב
חֶסֶד הַמְצֵא מְנוּחָה נְכוֹנָה תַּחַת
כַּנְפֵי הַשְּׁכִינָה אֶת־נִשְׁמַת ....

(for a male pet)

שֶׁהָלַךְ לְעוֹלָמוֹ וְיָנוּחַ בְּשָׁלוֹם עַל מִשְׁכָּבוֹ
אָמֵן

(for a female pet)

שֶׁהָלְכָה לְעוֹלָמָהּ. וְתָנוּחַ בְּשָׁלוֹם עַל
מִשְׁכָּבָהּ. אָמֵן

You may wish to pause here to remember your pet, and perhaps share some of those memories with family and friends.

God has given, and God has taken away; may God's name be praised.

יְיָ נָתַן וַיְיָ לָקָח יְהִי שֵׁם יְיָ מְבֹרָךְ.

The Eternal is gracious and full of compassion,

חַנּוּן וְרַחוּם יְהֹוָה

Slow to anger and of great mercy.

אֶרֶךְ אַפַּיִם וּגְדָל־חָסֶד.

The Eternal is good to all,

טוֹב־יְהֹוָה לַכֹּל

And God's tender mercies are over all God's works.

וְרַחֲמָיו עַל־כָּל־מַעֲשָׂיו.

For a female pet	*For a male pet*
Whenever I turned my key in the lock	Whenever I turned my key in the lock
I knew she would be waiting,	I knew he would be waiting,
Welcoming me home.	Welcoming me home.
Those days when the world seemed too cruel,	Those days when the world seemed too cruel,
Too hard, too fast, too lonely,	Too hard, too fast, too lonely,
She was always kind, easy, gentle,	He was always kind, easy, gentle,
The best listener.	The best listener.
She always made us laugh,	He always made us laugh,
Was the source of many stories:	Was the source of many stories:
'Remember the time she did this . . .?'	'Remember the time he did this . . .?'
'Remember the way she did that . . .?'	'Remember the way he did that . . .?'
And, though she kept her not-human mystery,	And, though he kept his not-human mystery,
Eating, sleeping, drifting, dreaming,	Eating, sleeping, drifting, dreaming,

Still we felt she let us know
her well.
And we told each other:
'She likes me doing that!'
'See how she smiles at me!'
'Isn't she sweet! Isn't she
silly!'
Feeling that she knew us
Better almost than we knew
ourselves.
That she taught us some-
thing
We were MEANT to learn.
Effortlessly loving, totally
loved.
Now, whenever I turn my
key in the lock,
I shall remember her wait-
ing,
Welcoming me home

Still we felt he let us know
him well.
And we told each other:
'He likes me doing that!'
'See how he smiles at me!'
'Isn't he sweet! Isn't he
silly!'
Feeling that he knew us
Better almost than we knew
ourselves.
That he taught us some-
thing
We were MEANT to learn.
Effortlessly loving, totally
loved.
Now, whenever I turn my
key in the lock,
I shall remember him wait-
ing,
Welcoming me home.

The soul of every living
being shall praise Your name,
Eternal our God, and the
spirit of all flesh shall acclaim
Your majesty for ever. From
everlasting to everlasting You
are God.

נִשְׁמַת כָּל־חַי תְּבָרֵךְ אֶת־שִׁמְךָ יְיָ
אֱלֹהֵינוּ וְרוּחַ כָּל־בָּשָׂר תְּפָאֵר וּתְרוֹמֵם
זִכְרְךָ מַלְכֵּנוּ תָּמִיד. מִן הָעוֹלָם
וְעַד־הָעוֹלָם אַתָּה אֵל.

Source of Creation and Life, in whose hand is the soul of
every living thing, thank You for the life of . . . who gave
me/us so much love and pleasure. May his/her memory be a
source of consolation always.

Magnified and sanctified be the great name of the One by whose will the world was created. May God's rule become effective in your lives, and in the life of the whole House of Israel. May it be so soon, and let us say: Amen.

יִתְגַּדַּל וְיִתְקַדַּשׁ שְׁמֵהּ רַבָּא בְּעָלְמָא דִי־בְרָא כִרְעוּתֵהּ וְיַמְלִיךְ מַלְכוּתֵהּ בְּחַיֵּיכוֹן וּבְיוֹמֵיכוֹן וּבְחַיֵּי דְכָל־בֵּית יִשְׂרָאֵל בַּעֲגָלָא וּבִזְמַן קָרִיב וְאִמְרוּ: אָמֵן.

May God's great name be praised to all eternity.

יְהֵא שְׁמֵהּ רַבָּא מְבָרַךְ לְעָלַם וּלְעָלְמֵי עָלְמַיָּא.

Blessed and praised; glorified, exalted and extolled; lauded, honoured and acclaimed be the name of the Holy One, who is ever to be praised, though far above the eulogies and songs of praise and consolation that human lips can utter; and let us say: Amen.

יִתְבָּרַךְ וְיִשְׁתַּבַּח וְיִתְפָּאַר וְיִתְרוֹמַם וְיִתְנַשֵּׂא, וְיִתְהַדַּר וְיִתְעַלֶּה וְיִתְהַלָּל שְׁמֵהּ דְּקֻדְשָׁא בְּרִיךְ הוּא לְעֵלָּא מִן־כָּל־בִּרְכָתָא וְשִׁירָתָא תֻּשְׁבְּחָתָא וְנֶחֱמָתָא דַּאֲמִירָן בְּעָלְמָא וְאִמְרוּ אָמֵן.

May great peace descend from heaven, and abundant life be granted, to us and all Israel; and let us say: Amen.

יְהֵא שְׁלָמָא רַבָּא מִן־שְׁמַיָּא וְחַיִּים עָלֵינוּ וְעַל־כָּל־יִשְׂרָאֵל וְאִמְרוּ אָמֵן.

May the Most High, Source of perfect peace, grant peace to us, to all Israel, and to all humanity, and let us say: Amen.

עֹשֶׂה שָׁלוֹם בִּמְרוֹמָיו הוּא יַעֲשֶׂה שָׁלוֹם עָלֵינוּ וְעַל כָּל־יִשְׂרָאֵל וְעַל כָּל־בְּנֵי־אָדָם וְאִמְרוּ: אָמֵן.

Let us bless the Source of Life, the Spirit of the universe.

נְבָרֵךְ אֶת־עֵין הַחַיִּים רוּחַ הָעוֹלָם.

Nevarech et Eyn HaChayim

Ne - va - rech et   eyn ha - cha - yim   ru - ach ha - o - lam

Ne   va   rech

Practicalities of burying your pet

Planning

It is worth giving some thought in advance to how you will handle the practical aspects of your pet's death. As with humans, there are two options, burial and cremation.

Burial

If you have space in your garden and the dead pet is not too big, you could undertake the burial of your pet yourself.

The pet can be placed in a simple cardboard box for burial. Make sure, however, that you dig the grave deeply enough (not less than three feet). There would be nothing more upsetting for you than to walk around your garden only to find that the local fox had raided your pet's recently dug grave.

Should you consider the option of garden burial, it may be worth remembering that you may not always live in that particular property. If you feel that you would like access to your pet's grave all your life then a pet cemetery may be more appropriate. Your local vet will have details of local pet cemeteries. I say local, but there are still only relatively few of these in the country and you may have to travel some distance to your nearest one.

Cremation

This is another option, perhaps to be followed by burial of the ashes in your garden, or alternatively, burying or scattering them in your pet's favourite place.

Unlike burial, cremation is not something to attempt yourself. There are a number of pet crematoria in the country and again, your local vet will be able to give you details of local pet cremation facilities.

References, allusions and sources

p. 161   'And God spoke to Noah', Genesis 9.8–11.
          'We patronize animals', Henry Beston, in Andrew Linzey and
          Dan Cohn-Sherbok, *After Noah. Animals and the Liberation
          of Theology*, Mowbray 1997, 137 n.39.
          'And God said', Genesis 9.12; 9.15.

p. 162   'We need another', Beston, in *After Noah*, 131.
          'Who sends forth', Psalm 104.10–13.
          'God, full of compassion', traditional from *Tzidduk ha-Din*,
          ULPS 1996, 15–16.

p. 163   'God has given', ibid., 18.
          'The Eternal is gracious', Ps.145.8–9.
          'Whenever I turned my key', poem composed for this liturgy by
          Sheila Yeger, Britol and West Progressive Jewish Congrega-
          tion, 1999.

p. 164   'The soul of every living being', traditional, from *Siddur Lev
          Chadash (SLC)*, ULPS 1995, 125.
          'Source of Creation of Life', Hadassah Davis, incorporating
          words from Job 12.10.

p. 165   'Magnified and sanctified', traditional, SLC, 524.
          Nevarech et eyn ha-chayyim by Marcia Lee Falk, in *Kol
          HaNeshamah*, Reconstructionist Press, Wyncote, PA 1994, 5.

          Music by Jon Stein, Bristol and West Progressive Jewish
          Congregation, 1998.

A Prayer during Depression

Alexandra Wright

Can prayer help those who are ill with depression? Sometimes, when we are feeling utterly helpless and powerless, it is the only recourse we possess. If you cannot pray with someone, then perhaps find a space to sit quietly and comfortably. The poet of this psalm tries to reach out to God from the depths of complete despair. The Psalmist's sense of worthlessness eclipses any feeling of self-value. Sometimes, all we can do is to wait for the journey to complete its course. Yet how painful and full of anguish such waiting can be – especially when the future seems so bleak.

Psalm 130

A Pilgrim Song

Out of the depths, I call to you, Eternal One,
O God, listen to my voice.
Let your ears hear the sound of my pleading.
God, if You should mark sins, Eternal, who could stand?
But with You there is forgiveness, and for this you are held in
awe.
I hope in the Eternal One, my soul has hope, and for God's
word I wait.
My soul waits for the Eternal One, more than watchers for
the morning, watching for the morning.
Israel hope in the Eternal One, for with the Eternal is constant
love,
and with God the immense capacity to set free.
It is God who redeems Israel from all their sins.

Source of Mercy, help me at this time of need. My soul is full of anguish and my spirit full of disquiet and terror. I see the world as though through a darkened glass. I cannot connect with anyone, not even those I am close to. Even the tender reaching out of friendship or love fills me with a sense of loss and sadness. Why does everything appear so distant from me? What is the path that lies ahead? Why am I so afraid of what will become of me? Why will my soul not rest in quietness and peace? Show me Your tenderness, forgiving God. Help me to open myself to Your presence; pour Your spirit into my soul that I may gain the patience to wait for this journey to continue. May I put my trust in You, and understand soon that I, too, am Your creation, formed in Your image and worthy to receive Your love and goodness. Amen.

Psalms to Help through Depression

Sybil Sheridan

My God, my God. Why have you abandoned me?

At the blackest hour, prayer may seem unthinkable. Who is the God who can allow such torment? What God can help this hopeless state? The merest thought of prayer brings with it waves of pain. All that is possible is to sit silent in the darkness. But prayer, once started, can bring its own healing; and on the journey back to life there is a comfort in knowing we are not alone.

The writers of these Psalms made the same journey. To trace their steps may be of help. Some psalms end in despair. Others tread the painful path from the depths of depression to hope and wholeness, but to the sufferer, the happy ending may seem contrived. Read what you can. Read to the point where you and the Psalmist part company. In time, with God's help, you too will move on and be able to share in the psalm of gratitude which ends this piece.

From Psalm 22

My God, my God. Why have you abandoned me?
Why so far from rescuing me – from the words that I scream out?

My God.
I cry out daily and you don't answer.
At night I have no peace of mind.
You are holy. Enthroned.
The praise of Israel – in you, our ancestors put their faith.
They trusted and you made them feel secure.

To you they cried out and were rescued
In you they trusted; they were not disappointed.

But I am a worm, not a person.
A disgrace to humanity, contemptible to people.
All who see me will laugh at me.
They will gape open mouthed and shake their heads.
'Open up to the Eternal, God will rescue you,
Will deliver you for such is God's pleasure.'
Because you delivered me from the womb
Because you fastened me to my mother's breast
I was thrown on to your protection at birth
From my mother's womb you became my God.
Don't distance yourself from me
For trouble is near, and there is no one to help.

Many bulls surround me, giant bulls encircle me
Their jaws are upon me, open – like a tearing, roaring lion.
I spill out like water, my bones pull apart.
My heart is like wax melting in the midst of me.
My strength dried up like a broken pot, my tongue sticking to
my gums;
and you sweep me to the dust of death.
For wild dogs surround me, a pack of evil ones encloses me
Like a lion on my hands and feet.
I count all my bones; they glance and gloat.
They divide my clothing; they gamble for my garments.
Adonai, please, do not be so distant,
My helper, be quick to aid me.
Deliver me from the sword that pierces my soul; from the dog
that clutches me.
Save me from the lion's jaws, and from the horns of wild
bulls.
Answer me!

I will recount your qualities to my companions;
In the midst of the community I will sing your praises.
You who fear God, give praise; all the descendants of Jacob,
give honour.

Stand in awe you descendants of Israel.
For God does not scorn, and God does not spurn the plight of
the afflicted
There is no hiding of God's face from you; when you cry for
help, God listens . . .

Psalm 77

My voice cries out to God and I scream aloud.
My voice cries out to God that God will listen to me.
In the day in my distress, I seek my God.
At night, my hand is stretched out it will not rest.
My soul will not be comforted.

I recall God and moan in confusion. I complain; my soul is
overwhelmed.
You have seized my eyelids. I am so disturbed I cannot speak.
I think over earlier days, years long gone.
I remember my song in the night.
I argue with myself, I search in my soul.
Has my God rejected me for ever? Am I no longer wanted?
Is God's enduring love now nothing? Are God's words
finished for evermore?
Has God forgotten how to pity?
Has God in anger shut down compassion?
And I said, it is my fault that the right hand of the Most High
has changed.

I recall God's actions and I recall your wonders of ages past.
I will concentrate on all your work and discuss your acts.
God, your way is in holiness; what deity is greater?
You are the God who works miracles, you made known your
strength to the nations.
You saved with your outstretched hand the children of Jacob
and Joseph.
Waters saw you, God, waters saw you and raged;
Even the deepest depths quaked.
Dense clouds poured forth water; thin clouds gave voice,

Inflamed arrows flying about.
The sound of your thunder echoed in tornado; lightning
illumined the world,
The ground trembled and quaked.
Your way is in the sea and your path in mighty waters,
but your footprints are not known.
You have guided your people like a flock by the hand of
Moses and Aaron.

אָנָּא אֵל נָא רְפָא נָא לִי
Ana El na r'fah na li
God, please, heal, please, me.

Psalm 88

Eternal, God of my rescuing when I cry out in the night
against you.
Let my prayer come before you, incline your ear to my cry
Because my soul is full with anguish and my life touches
death.
I was considered in the deepest depths, a person without help
Wandering freely with the dead, like those killed; buried in
their grave
Who are no longer remembered and cut off from you.
You have put me in the bottommost pit in the darkness in the
depths.
Your rage weighs heavily on me, your waves bear down on
me.
You have distanced those that know me from me,
You have made me disgusting to them; shut in, I can't escape.
My eyes are failing because of my suffering;
I have called to you, Eternal One, every day;
I have stretched out my hands to you.

Do you create miracles for the dead? Do ghosts rise to
thank you?
Is your love talked of in the grave? Your faith in ruined
places?

Are your wonders known in darkness? Your righteousness in
oblivion?
But I, to you Eternal One, I have called for help and in the
morning early my prayer has come to you.
Why, then, Adonai do you reject me? Why hide your face
from me?
Afflicted am I and chastened from childhood. I bore your
tremendous terrors.
Your anger advanced over me; your dread has annihilated me.
They surround me like waters all day long; they encompass
me together.
You have distanced from me lover and friend; those that were
known to me melt into darkness.

Psalm 13

How long, Eternal One will you forget me . . . for ever?
How long will you hide your face from me?
How long will I bear this burden on my soul; this grief daily
in my heart?
How long will my enemy rise above me?
Look at me! answer me! Eternal, my God.
Light my eyes, lest I sleep to death, lest my enemy say 'I have
ended it'
My tormentors rejoice that I have stumbled.

But I, I trust in your love. My heart rejoices in your saving
power.
I will sing to the Eternal, for he has been good to me.

הֲשִׁיבֵנוּ יהוה אֵלֶיךָ וְנָשׁוּבָה חַדֵּשׁ יָמֵינוּ כְּקֶדֶם

*Hashiveinu Adonai eilekha v'nashuva hadesh yameinu
k'kedem*
Bring us back and we shall return, renew us as we were of old[2]

Psalm 130

From the depths I cry to you Adonai,
O God listen to my voice.
Let your ears be attentive to the sound of my supplication.
If you keep account of sins, God, who would stand?
But with you is forgiveness, that you be held in awe.
I hoped, Adonai; my soul has hoped and for God's word I
waited.
My soul is for my God more than watchmen for the morning
watching for the morning.
Israel, wait for the Eternal One, for with the Eternal is
constant love and great capacity to set free.
It is God who will free Israel from all her sins.

Psalm 57

Pity me, God, pity me, for in you my soul seeks refuge.
In the shelter of your wings find protection until destruction
passes.
I will cry to the God on High, to the deity who ends this for
me
God will reach down from heaven and save me
Scorning those who crush me, *Selah*. God will send his love
and his truth.
My soul is in the midst of lions, I lie down with them;
Fired up against the children of men, their teeth are spears and
arrows,
Their tongues a sharp sword.
Be exalted upon the heavens, God; upon all the earth be your
glory.

They prepared a net for my feet, my soul bowed down.
They dug a pit for me, then they fell into it.
My heart is strong, God, my heart is strong
I will sing and give praise.
Awake, my esteem, awake!

With harp and lyre I will arouse the dawn.
I will thank you among the peoples, my guide,
I will sing praises to you among the nations
For your love is as great as the heavens, and your truth
extends to the clouds
Be exalted upon the heavens, God; upon all the earth be your
glory.

בָּרוּךְ אַתָּה יְיָ רוֹפֵא הַחוֹלִים
Barukh attah Adonai rofei ha-holim
Blessed are you, Eternal One, who heals the sick.

A Rabbi's Experience of Illness

Amanda Golby

I sometimes smile to myself when I think that 'Can I take a service at 11.00?' was my immediate response to receiving a telephone call late on a Thursday evening in May 1997. The call was from my surgeon to say that, totally unexpectedly, the pathology result from the analysis of a breast lump revealed malignancy. He wanted to see me at 9.00 a.m. on Saturday morning. (His actual words were more to the effect that 'it's rather serious, not what we were expecting'.)

Apparently some people remember what they were wearing at such a moment. I don't, but I know that I was preparing a sermon, and my first thought was to be concerned about Shabbat services. The response to my question was 'What do you think?', and I quickly realized I would not be able to. So I arranged for last-minute substitutes, saying I was unwell. I really did not want most people to know until I had had the appointment. I had that day received a request to renew a journal subscription. The most economical way was to renew for three years, and I recall thinking that I clearly would not need it for such a long time.

What was my reaction on that Thursday night? Well, I rang the few people whom I wanted to know immediately and was comforted by offers to come over and to accompany me to my appointment. Needless to say I had very little sleep that night, and found myself thinking, 'Why me, what have I done wrong?' I even had such crazy thoughts as that perhaps Progressive Judaism is not legitimate, perhaps women should not be rabbis!

I must say that those thoughts did not last very long, and perhaps a more appropriate question was, 'Why not me?' After all, one in twelve women is diagnosed as having breast cancer, and all the signs were that I would be cured. Further surgery, thankfully, revealed that nothing had spread to the lymph glands. I had radiotherapy and immediately after diagnosis was prescribed the drug Tamoxifen. Statistically, I am likely to live a long life. Perhaps with more years ahead than those I have already lived. I could die in my nineties of something totally unrelated. Yet, it is possible that I could be one of the unlucky women, and I know I shall feel more reassured when I reach the five-year mark and all remains well.

Strangely, almost from the beginning, I have been strongly aware of a sense of gratitude. Not 'Why me?' as a punishment, but 'Why me?' as a learning experience. A way of learning how to go from being the carer to the one who needs to be cared for, as a way of strengthening my faith, my rabbinate. Yet these thoughts also present difficulties. I go back to that Saturday morning, definitely Saturday, not Shabbat, when things were explained to me. There was the painful task of telling my parents, and I knew how distressed they would be. I am grateful to my brother and sister-in-law who told them. I also had to discuss arrangements for the congregation during my period of sick leave. I remained very calm throughout this time, and I believe that this led others to behave similarly. I remember the synagogue Chairman and Secretary going through my diary; it was all so very 'normal'. I was totally overwhelmed by the support I received from family, friends, congregation and colleagues, and that sense of feeling supported has continued.

I live alone and had always regarded myself, away from the very public life of a congregational rabbi, as a very private person. As a rabbi there is something of a paradox in that one knows many details of the private lives of many people, while choosing what one reveals of oneself. Certainly my illness caused me to reveal far more than I would have wanted to. There was no choice, though, and again, it proved to be a most important experience.

There were practical things. Suddenly, while in hospital, I realized that I would need laundry done and other practical help during the long weeks of treatment and convalescence. I learned to accept that help and am grateful to all those who gave it so willingly. There were also emotional difficulties. For a brief time I did not think that I would be able again to lead the congregation in prayer. I worried about reading aloud the words in the service, not least prayers for the sick, knowing that so many of them would have a renewed significance. It was not easy, but it became easier. The first service I attended as a congregant was difficult, but I realized I was pleased to be back. On that occasion I was somewhat taken aback, as we came to the *kaddish*, to hear an 'inner voice' telling me that I must say *kaddish* for all those who have died of breast cancer. That still remains important for me.

My goal was to start back for the High Holydays. With hindsight, it was too soon. I needed more convalescent time afterwards, but it was another important learning experience. Each year of my rabbinate I have made the point that while I regard fasting an important part of Yom Kippur, Jewish law forbids anyone to fast whose health may be affected by it. It was difficult to acknowledge that I could not fast, and harder still when I realized that I could be in the synagogue for only the morning service. A year later, I was so grateful at how much progress I had made that I could be in the synagogue all day, and I was genuinely not bothered by, again, being unable to fast.

Certainly I felt that my religious faith and all the experiences of pastoral work were very helpful. At the same time they were a source of difficulty. A few weeks ago there was a delay in getting back test results. Until I was reassured, I was full of panic. It was as though I had learned nothing in the previous eighteen months. I am told that for many people such anxiety continues for years. I definitely feel that knowing even the worst is better than knowing nothing, and I am truly able to share with others my personal knowledge of the stress of that waiting time.

There was another learning experience, too. Like most of my colleagues I used to work long hours, finding it difficult to say 'no'. Some would say I still do, but I have very definitely changed in the way I use my time. My first responsibility is to look after myself, as it is only then that I am able to look after others. As I said at the start, I smile when I think of my immediate response to diagnosis, 'Can I take a service at 11.00?' Now I realize that no matter how much I am valued as myself and in my work as a rabbi, my own personal health needs must come first. Rabbis are of the greatest importance to their congregations, ideally valued and respected by them, but we are not indispensable.

Yes, I believe my experience has made me a better rabbi. How has it affected me as a Jewish woman though? In the previous volume of essays by women rabbis, *Hear Our Voice*, I wrote about the significance for women of *Rosh Hodesh*, the new moon – the subject of my Leo Baeck College thesis. It saddens me that the oestrogen-suppressing effects of Tamoxifen mean I no longer have a monthly cycle that can be paralleled with that of the moon. Yes, it would have happened in any event in a few years. Yes, *Rosh Hodesh* has now regained its special significance for me, but I did spend several months wondering whether I had lost my sense of connection with those special days.

Over the years I have wished numerous people a '*r'fuah sh'lemah*', sometimes thought to mean a speedy recovery, 'get well soon'. Being the recipient of those words made me fully appreciate the ancient wisdom of the two-fold wish *r'fuat ha-nefesh u-r'fuat ha-guf*, a perfect healing of body and soul. Both elements are necessary, and I also feel convinced that a perfect healing may not mean the same as a complete recovery. I feel it is more fully accepting and coming to terms with the experience and incorporating it into one's life.

What of the future? Clearly I hope that the cancer experience will become a distant memory, even though medication and check-ups will remain part of my life for the foreseeable future. Yet, I hope that the lessons remain with me, to strengthen my personal and professional life, whether that life is long or short. No, I don't make the most of every single minute; that would not be humanly possible. But I do have a new appreciation of the significance of life. I am particularly aware of the truth of the seeming paradox contained in the words of the eleventh-century Spanish poet and philosopher, Solomon Ibn Gabirol:

Plan for this world as if you were to live for ever, plan for the world to come as if you were to die tomorrow.

In conclusion, I think back to that Thursday evening telephone call. When I received it, I was writing a sermon for Shabbat *Behar*,[1] which was to be about the significance of jubilees. Now, the verse from the *sedra* that comes to mind is from Leviticus 25.23:

But the land must not be sold beyond reclaim, for the land is Mine,
you are but strangers resident with Me.

We do not own the land absolutely, though too often we are tempted to behave as though we do. Likewise, we do not own our lives absolutely, though we too often behave as though we do. Illness has reinforced for me the significance of the gift of life, the responsibilities we have. Whatever my future brings, I pray that I will be privileged to remember that, to live that and, where possible, use my experiences to help others.

(Dedicated, with grateful thanks, to all who, in different ways, have provided help; particularly CAS and MAJS.)

Beginning a Religious Response to Mastectomy

Sylvia Rothschild

The diagnosis of breast cancer is one that all women dread, bringing with it a maelstrom of thoughts and emotions – fear of pain, of death, of disfigurement; a sense of betrayal by one's own body; worries about femininity; about sexuality, about relationships; loss of control over one's own person.

To lose a breast is so much more than the loss of a body part; the breast is integral to our perceptions of ourselves as woman – lover, mother, nurturer, life-giver. The breast is the symbol of our power and our strength. A liturgy which helps us to ground ourselves in an encounter with God at this time, and which also allows us to reclaim and transform our female strength so as to continue to live a life of quality and empowerment, is greatly needed.

A meditation before mastectomy

Hear the voice of a woman, the anguish of the daughter of Zion, sobbing and spreading out her hands, saying, 'Woe is me, for my soul faints.'
I am pained at my very heart, I cannot be peaceful and destruction follows upon destruction.
I looked on the earth and behold it was waste and empty; at the heavens, and they had no light.
I looked on the mountains and behold, they trembled, with all the hills moving to and fro.
I looked on, and behold, there was no one, and all the birds of the heavens had fled.
I looked on, and behold the fruitful place was a wilderness.[1]

God, known to us El Shaddai, Source of all power and strength, who enfolds and supports us, in whose image I am made, be with me at this time of terror and desolation which has fallen upon me so suddenly. Remember me and be mindful of me. I am fainting away. My sun has gone down while it is still day, I am confused and confounded.[2] My heart moans within me, my eyes are a fountain of tears. Help me to see that my world still exists, my life is still to be lived, my self is not destroyed.

Now that I must begin a journey of damage and destruction, of pain and grief;

– help me to keep faith with those who seek to cure me,

– help me to trust the healing brought about through such an injury,

– teach me to hold fast to the person I am and to let go of the fear and loneliness which threaten to overwhelm me.

Be with me, El Shaddai, You who know the meaning of my life,

– give me strength and courage, trust and hope,

– cover me in the shelter of your wings,

– hold me to Your breast and comfort me.

Deliver me from my illness, I run to your sheltering presence, for you are my God, your spirit is good.

For Your own name, God, cause me to live most fully,

For your own righteousness bring my soul out from this trouble.

And in your great mercy cut me away from my adversaries, destroy all who afflict my soul, for I am Your servant.[3]

Psalm 139

To the One who grants victory, by David, a Psalm

God, You have searched me, and so you know me,
You, You know me as I sit quietly and also when I decide to act.
You anticipate my thoughts before they are formed.
You watched my journey and the places where I stop

travelling and are familiar with all my ways.

For there is not a word on my tongue, yet You already know it, all of it.

You have confined me between the past and the future, and have laid Your hand on me.

This knowledge is too wonder-filled for me, too high, I am not capable of it.

Where could I go from Your spirit?

Where could I flee from Your presence?

If I could climb to heaven, You are there.

If I were to make my bed in the lowest depths – there You are.

Were I to take up the wings of the morning, were I to live at the end of the sea, even there your hand would lead me, Your right hand would hold me.

If I were to say 'Surely darkness will cover me from You', then the night would become light around me.

Even darkness will not be dark to you, but night as bright as day, the darkness like the light.

For you created my innermost being when you kept me hidden in my mother's womb.

I thank you for the awesome wonder that I am, for the wonder of Your works, my soul knows it well.

My essence was not hidden from you when I was made in secret, when I was made in the lowest parts of the earth.

Your eyes saw my essence while still unformed, all is written down in Your book.

The days were determined, and one among them was appointed.

God, how precious are your thoughts to me, how overwhelming even their beginnings.

I will count them – they increase more than the sand, yet if I reached the end still I am with You.

If, God, You will destroy the wicked – depart from me, men of blood,

who, having pronounced Your name in vanity, deprive me of hope.

Those who hate You God, do I not hate them?

It is with the uprisings against You that I contend.
With utmost hatred I count those as my enemies.
Search me, God, and know my heart.
Try me, and know my thoughts,
and see if there is any way in me that is to be renounced,
and lead me in the way of eternity.

בְּשֵׁם יְיָ אֱלֹהֵי יִשְׂרָאֵל מִימִינִי מִיכָאֵל, וּמִשְּׂמֹאלִי גַּבְרִיאֵל, וּמִלְּפָנַי אוּרִיאֵל,
וּמֵאֲחוֹרַי רְפָאֵל וְעַל רֹאשִׁי שְׁכִינַת אֵל.

B'sheim Adonai elohei Yisrael, mi-y'mini Mihael u-mi-s'moli Gavriel; u-mi-l'fanai Uriel, u-mei-ahorai Raphael; ve-al roshi Sh'khinat El.

In the name of Adonai, God of Israel, may Michael the protection of God be at my right hand, and Gavriel the power of God at my left; before me Uriel the light of God; behind me Raphael the healing of God; and above my head Sh'khinat El, the dwelling presence of God.

Amen.

Healing

Marcia Plumb

'May the One who blessed our ancestors, Abraham, Isaac and Jacob, Sarah, Rebecca, Leah and Rachel, send a complete healing of body and mind, and blessing to our loved one who is ill . . .'

This article includes personal and communal rituals and prayers for healing. The healing that I speak of is not one which involves laying on of hands or examples of that ilk. When I refer to healing, I speak of the traditional Jewish path towards physical and emotional health via prayer.

Often, in prayers or in our hearts, we ask God to heal the one we love from the illness he or she suffers. Implicitly we are asking God to perform a miracle in some cases, or in others, we turn God's attention to our loved one or ourselves and 'fix' whatever physically or emotionally is wrong. We ask God to cure the disease. Naturally, we want pain and suffering to disappear. In asking God to take it away, however, we can miss a point of healing.

Healing does not always mean that the illness is cured, however much we might want that to be the case. The reality is that we may not get well, or even better. When we say prayers for healing, we must at the same time acknowledge that complete health may not come. Healing can mean that illness is removed, but it can also mean that deeper self-understanding is gained, or reconciliation with family is achieved as a result of the illness. Paul Cowan, the author of *An Orphan in Jerusalem*, once said that his leukaemia, from which he later died, taught him for the first time how much he was loved. He had never felt the love that others had for him, and had always felt deeply alone within himself, until he became ill. Then he finally was able to receive the love that others gave him. He was grateful to his illness for this gift. For him, although his physical life was shortened and etched with pain, his emotional and spiritual life was greatly enhanced and deepened.

After a healing service at my synagogue, a congregant with a very ill partner pointed out to me that asking only for renewed physical health was misleading because sometimes people do not get better. Healing, she said, also meant enlightenment, or support and strength to carry on, or lessons learned. In other words, illness and suffering can provide powerful lessons, and greater self-love and love for others. A sixteenth-century Japanese potter would never allow his apprentices to discard a cracked pot. He would say, 'Honour the workings of chance in your creation.' He would often instruct them to outline the cracks with tracings of gold. So too illness, or other 'cracks' in our souls or bodies, although unwanted and sources of pain, can be honoured as teachers for us. It is not God that can teach us these lessons. In order to gain greater understanding of ourselves in relation to our illness or suffering, it is we who must do the work to open our hearts or minds.

As Debbie Friedman says, '. . . (Mishnah) *B'rakhot*: Chapter 9 states that it is incumbent upon us to bless what is good and what is not good. To bless what is good is a cinch, to bless what is bad is hard. Blessing what is bad or evil is the first step to admitting the adverse impact of an event on one's life, and therefore, the first step toward healing.' I wish my car accident, and the pain that followed, had never happened. However, the lessons I learned about myself and my role in this world changed my life, and had consequences for my family as well as myself. I think of a Jewish story: A woman dies and appears before the Holy One who asks, 'Show me your wounds.' The woman says, 'I have no wounds.' Says the Holy One, 'Was there nothing worth fighting for?'

And another: There once was a pious Jewish family – a mother, father and son – who, though lacking in material wealth, found great riches in each other, in their traditions, and in their beliefs. Alas, as time went on, the mother developed a serious illness, one which increasingly prevented her from doing all the things that helped make her life and that of her family so deep and satisfying. It was only a matter of weeks before she was too weak to do any preparation for Shabbat, and though her husband and son willingly did their best to handle all the shopping, cleaning and cooking, sadness and despair weighed heavily over the house.

Father prayed and prayed to get some help and guidance. He prayed for healing for his wife. One week, he heard a voice tell him to invite a beggar into his home for Shabbat and provide this needy person with every manner of food and comfort. He instructed his son to help him with this, explaining that this *mitzvah* would surely bring healing.

The son exerted himself immensely – preparing a clean room for the guest, cooking meals, and responding to the beggar's every request, of which there were many. By late on Shabbat day, the son's resentment grew so strong that he exploded in rage to his father: 'Why, what good is this? Mother is in pain, fading away and this ungrateful man is treating us like slaves!'

Calmly his father reminded him of the voice which promised that this *mitzvah* would bring healing to the home. 'What healing?!' yelled the son, 'Mother has not recovered – she may even have worsened!' 'Not her, my son – him,' said the father. From the next room, the mother's voice called out. The son and father came running, and when they drew near to her bed, she said, 'What a beautiful Shabbat this has been. May we merit many more.'

We may pray to God to take away our pain or illness. But God's 'job' is not necessarily to do so. We can see God's role as helping us understand and find meaning in what happens to us. Healing can often mean that we gain understanding and other lessons through our pain, or that we learn to live with it.

Rabbi Nancy Flam, of the Healing Center in New York, reminds us that God created limits as part of creation. For example, night and day were created so that time would pass. Life and death are part of the imposition of limits upon us in our world. We are physical beings, and so are vulnerable to disease, injury and decay. This fact is part of God's holy design. No matter how much we wish it, we cannot escape that truth. But we can learn how to endure the sometimes excruciatingly painful limits and losses of creation.

Compassion and support from others can help us to rise above the pain we feel when ill or bereaved. Prayer, with others or privately, can inspire and comfort us. The following prayers can constitute a healing service. They can also be said privately. A healing service differs from a standard daily or Shabbat worship in that it has no formal structure. It is in the nature of healing services that there is no formal beginning, middle or end. It is simply a collection of prayers that concern healing. In the context of such a service, it is common to study a text that focuses on some aspect of healing. Some examples of texts to study include Numbers 12.10–16; the *Hashkiveinu* prayer in the Shabbat evening service; the *Vidui* prayer, which can be found in *Mourning in Halakhah* by Greenberg; Talmud Rosh Hashana 18a; Talmud Ketubot 103b–104a.

Prayers that can be used in a communal setting or service

שְׁמַע קוֹלֵנוּ יְיָ אֱלֹהֵינוּ חוּס וְרַחֵם עָלֵינוּ וְקַבֵּל בְּרַחֲמִים וּבְרָצוֹן אֶת-תְּפִלָּתֵנוּ כִּי אֵל שׁוֹמֵעַ תְּפִלּוֹת וְתַחֲנוּנִים אָתָּה.

Sh'ma koleinu Adonai eloheinu hus v'rahem aleinu v'kabbel b'rahamim u-v'ratson et t'fillateinu ki el shomeia t'fillot v'tahanunim attah.

Adonai our God, hear our voice. Have compassion on us, pity us, accept our prayer with loving favour. You listen to entreaty and prayer.

Asher Yatzar – *to be said in appreciation of the workings of our bodies when health is good or restored, or in prayer for good health.*

בָּרוּךְ אַתָּה יְיָ אֱלֹהֵינוּ מֶלֶךְ הָעוֹלָם אֲשֶׁר יָצַר אֶת-הָאָדָם בְּחָכְמָה וּבָרָא בוֹ נְקָבִים נְקָבִים חֲלוּלִים חֲלוּלִים גָּלוּי וְיָדוּעַ לִפְנֵי כִסֵּא כְבוֹדֶךָ שֶׁאִם יִפָּתֵחַ אֶחָד מֵהֶם אוֹ יִסָּתֵם אֶחָד מֵהֶם אִי אֶפְשַׁר לְהִתְקַיֵּם וְלַעֲמוֹד לְפָנֶיךָ. בָּרוּךְ אַתָּה יְיָ רוֹפֵא כָל-בָּשָׂר וּמַפְלִיא לַעֲשׂוֹת.

Blessed are you, our Eternal God, Creator of the Universe, who has made our bodies in wisdom, creating openings, arteries, glands, and organs, marvellous in structure, intricate in design. Should but one of them, by being blocked or opened, fail to function, it would be difficult to stand before You. Wondrous Fashioner and Sustainer of life, Source of our health and our strength, we give You thanks and praise.

Elohai Neshamah – *to be said in appreciation of the soul or spirit that is housed within our bodies; to be said when we learn something or gain an understanding that enhances ourselves or our lives, or when we struggle with the death of someone we love or our own.*

אֱלֹהַי נְשָׁמָה שֶׁנָּתַתָּ בִּי טְהוֹרָה הִיא אַתָּה בְרָאתָהּ אַתָּה יְצַרְתָּהּ אַתָּה נְפַחְתָּהּ בִּי וְאַתָּה
מְשַׁמְּרָהּ בְּקִרְבִּי וְאַתָּה עָתִיד לִטְּלָהּ מִמֶּנִּי וּלְהַחֲזִירָהּ בִּי לֶעָתִיד לָבֹא. כָּל־זְמַן
שֶׁהַנְּשָׁמָה בְקִרְבִּי מוֹדֶה אֲנִי לְפָנֶיךָ יְיָ אֱלֹהַי וֵאלֹהֵי אֲבוֹתַי וְאִמּוֹתַי רִבּוֹן כָּל־הַמַּעֲשִׂים
אֲדוֹן כָּל־הַנְּשָׁמוֹת. בָּרוּךְ אַתָּה יְיָ הַמַּחֲזִיר נְשָׁמוֹת.

My God, the soul You have placed within me is pure. You have created it, You have formed it, You have breathed it into me. You preserve it within me, and You will one day take it from me and restore it to me in time to come. So long as my soul is within me, I give thanks before You, my God and God of all generations. Blessed are You, God who restores my soul each day, that I may once again awaken.

A Litany for Healing – to be said by all present responsively, with spontaneous personal additions at the end from those present if they wish.

When Miriam was sick, her brother Moses prayed, 'Oh God, heal her now please!' We join in this responsive prayer based on Moses' words:
We pray for those who are now ill.
    Source of Life, we pray: Heal them.
We pray for those who are affected by illness, anguish, sadness and pain.
    Heal them.

Grant courage to those whose bodies, holy proof of Your creative goodness, are violated by the illness and pain of illness or suffering.

Encourage them.

Grant strength and compassion to families and friends who give their loving care and support and help to overcome despair.

Strengthen them.

Grant wisdom to those who probe the deepest complexities of Your world as they labour in the search for treatments and cures.

Inspire them.

Grant clarity of vision and strength of purpose to the leaders of our institutions and our government. May they be moved to act with justice and compassion and find the courage to overcome fear, hatred and apathy toward illnesses.

Guide them.

Grant insight to us, that we may understand that whenever death comes, we must accept it – but that before it comes, we must resist it, by prolonging life, and by making our life worthy as long as it is lived.

Bless and heal us all.

Prayer for Those who Help

May the One who blessed our ancestors be present to those who provide help for the ill and troubled among us. May they be filled with fortitude and courage, endowed with sympathy and compassion, as they give strength to those at their side. May they fight against despair, and continue to find within themselves the will to reach out to those in need. And in their love of others, may they know the blessing of community, and the blessing of renewed faith.

Mi She – beirakh – *Prayer for Healing*

May the One who blessed our ancestors, Abraham and Sarah, Isaac and Rebecca, Jacob, Rachel and Leah, bless ...... along

with all the ill amongst us. Grant insight to those who bring
healing, compassion and faith to those who are sick; love and
strength to us and all who love them. God, let your Spirit rest
upon all who are ill and comfort them. May they and we soon
know a time of complete healing, a healing of body and a healing of the spirit and let us say: Amen.

Traditional prayer for healing

יְהִי רָצוֹן מִלְּפָנֶיךָ יְיָ אֱלֹהֵינוּ וֵאלֹהֵי אֲבוֹתֵינוּ שֶׁתִּשְׁלַח לִי מְהֵרָה רְפוּאָה שְׁלֵמָה
רְפוּאַת הַנֶּפֶשׁ וּרְפוּאַת הַגּוּף בְּתוֹךְ שְׁאָר הַחוֹלִים. בָּרוּךְ אַתָּה יְיָ רוֹפֵא הַחוֹלִים.

May it be Your will, Eternal God, and God of our ancestors,
speedily to grant a complete healing from heaven, a healing of
body and a healing of soul and mind to me and all who are in
need. I praise you O God, the Source of healing.

Conclusion of healing service: The Priestly Benediction

יְבָרֶכְךָ יְהֹוָה וְיִשְׁמְרֶךָ: יָאֵר יְהֹוָה פָּנָיו אֵלֶיךָ וִיחֻנֶּךָּ: יִשָּׂא יְהֹוָה פָּנָיו אֵלֶיךָ וְיָשֵׂם לְךָ
שָׁלוֹם:

May God bless you and keep you. May you feel God's presence
in your life. May God look with favour upon you. May God
look upon you and give you peace.

Prayers for private meditation
*(these prayers and psalms can also be said in a communal
setting)*

רְפָאֵנִי יְיָ וְאֵרָפֵא הוֹשִׁיעֵנִי וְאִוָּשֵׁעָה.

Heal me, O God, and I shall be healed: Save me and I shall be
saved.

Psalm 139

O God, You have searched me and know me well. You understand all my thoughts and every word upon my tongue. Your
presence surrounds me; You touch me with Your hand. It
exceeds my own perception; it is a wonder beyond imagining.
If I say, 'Let darkness hide me and turn the light to darkness,'

even the darkness is not dark for You; the night shines forth like day; the darkness is as light for You. How precious are Your thoughts to me, O God, how endless their number, more numerous than the grains of sand. When I awake, I am still with You. Search my soul, O God, and know my heart. If there is sorrow in me, lead me in Your everlasting ways.

My God, I thank You for my life, my soul and my body; for my name, my sexual and affectional nature, for my way of thinking and talking. Help me realize that in my qualities I am unique in the world, and that no one like me has ever lived; for if there had ever before been someone like me, I would not have needed to exist. Help me make perfect my own ways of loving and caring, that by becoming complete in my own way, I can honour Your name, and help bring about the coming of the Messianic Age.

Esah Einai – Psalm 121

אֶשָּׂא עֵינַי אֶל-הֶהָרִים מֵאַיִן יָבֹא עֶזְרִי:
עֶזְרִי מֵעִם יְהֹוָה עֹשֵׂה שָׁמַיִם וָאָרֶץ:

I lift up my eyes to the hills; from where will come my help? My help is from God, Creator of heaven and earth.

Psalm 86

Incline Your ear, Adonai, answer me, for I am poor and needy. Preserve my life, for I am steadfast;
O You, O God, deliver Your servant who trusts in You.
Have mercy on me, Adonai, for I call to You all day long;
bring joy to Your servant's life, for on You, Adonai, I set my hope.
For You, Adonai, are good and forgiving, abounding in steadfast love to all who call on You.
Give ear, Adonai, to my prayer; heed my plea for mercy. In my time of trouble I call You, for You will answer me.

A compilation from the Psalms

Unto You, Adonai, I call, and unto You I make supplication.

Hear, Eternal, and be gracious unto me; Adonai, be my Helper.
You heal the broken-hearted and bind up their wounds.
You, who have done great things, O God, who is like You?
God, hear my prayers, and let my cry come to You.
Do not hide from me in the day of my distress. Turn to me and
speedily answer my prayer.
Heal me, Adonai, and I shall be healed; save me and I shall be
saved.
For You are my praise.

A prayer for forgiveness

*This prayer offers us an opportunity to ask forgiveness for the
behaviour which we would like to change in ourselves and to
give us a chance to ask for forgiveness from God, which can
help us in our healing.*

God, being merciful, grants atonement from sin and does not
destroy.
God, do not withhold Your compassion from us. Let Your love
and faithfulness constantly shield us. Who could endure, O
God, if You kept count of every sin? But forgiveness is Yours,
that we may worship You. Deal with us not in accordance with
our sins; punish us not in accordance with our transgressions.
When our sins testify against us, forgive us because of Your
mercy and our merit. Remember Your compassion and Your
loving kindness. O divine Presence, help us, answer us when
we call. Remember Your everlasting love for us. *Avinu
Malkeinu*, answer us graciously, though we have not the
strength to ask fully. Heed our plea, remember the covenant
with our ancestors and with us, and help us. Amen.

הֲשִׁיבֵנוּ יְהֹוָה אֵלֶיךָ וְנָשׁוּבָה חַדֵּשׁ יָמֵינוּ כְּקֶדֶם.
*Hashiveinu Adonai aleykha, v'nashuva haddeish yameinu
k'kedem.*
Turn us toward You, God, and we will return. Renew our days
as at the beginning.

Oseh Shalom

עֹשֶׂה שָׁלוֹם בִּמְרוֹמָיו הוּא יַעֲשֶׂה שָׁלוֹם עָלֵינוּ וְעַל־כָּל־יִשְׂרָאֵל וְעַל־כָּל־בְּנֵי אָדָם וְאִמְרוּ
אָמֵן

Oseh shalom bimromav hu ya'aseh shalom aleinu, ve-al kol Yisrael, ve-al kol b'nei adam, ve-imru amen.

May the One who makes peace in the heavens let peace descend upon us, upon all Israel and all the world, and let us say: Amen.[1]

Notes

Preface

1. Joel Lurie Grishaver, *The Bonding of Isaac*, Alef Design Group 1997, 71.
2. We would welcome people's responses and information about how they use and change the rituals. The editors can be reached c/o Leo Baeck College, East End Road, London N3 2 SY.

Expanding the Borders of Prayer

1. Hebrew for the description of the world before creation, implying chaotic and unformed.
2. Exodus 35.3.

Women, Prayer and Ritual in the Bible

1. H.W. and F.G. Fowler (eds), *Concise Oxford Dictionary of Current English*, Oxford University Press 1998.
2. Lionel Blue, *To Heaven with Scribes and Pharisees*, Darton, Longman and Todd, London 1975.
3. See Judith Plaskow, 'The Wife/Sister Stores: Dilemmas of the Jewish Feminist', in Diana L. Eck and Devaki Jain, *Speaking of Faith*, The Women's Press 1986.
4. *Yalkut Shmoni* 80, 'And Hannah prayed' (I Samuel 2.1). From this we learn that women are required to pray, for Hannah was reciting *Shemonah Esreh* (the daily liturgy).
5. Shoshana Gelerenter-Leibowitz, 'Growing up Lubavitch', in *Daughters of the King*, ed. Susan Grossman and Ricka Haut, JPS 1992.
6. Midrash Rabbah Song of Songs II, 41.
7. See Penina Adelman, 'Home and Homeland: A Light Returns to Sarah's Tent', in *Lifecycles* 2, ed. Orenstein and Litman, Woodstock: Jewish Lights 1997.
8. E.g. Rachel weeping for her children: '. . . Accept therefore the weeping of holy Rachel together with our tears so that we may merit to behold the return quickly in our own day', in *A Book of Jewish*

Women's Prayers, selected and edited by Norman Tarnor, New
Jersey: Aronson 1995, 116.

9. Micah 6.4.
10. See Rachel Montagu, 'Women as Role Models in the Hebrew Bible',
    in Sybil Sheridan (ed.), *Hear Our Voice*, SCM Press 1994, 52.
11. Sybil Sheridan, 'The Song of Solomon's Wife', citing Schlomo
    Gotiein, in ibid., 70.
12. Judges 11.
13. See Rachel Montagu, 'Women as Role Models' (n.10), 164–5.
14. Lowell K. Handy, 'The Appearance of Pantheon in Judah', in Diana
    Vikander Adelman (ed.), *The Triumph of Elohim*, Kok Pharos 1995,
    33. Asphodel Long, personal communication; the archaeological
    view of who was worshipped as God in ancient Israel is quite differ-
    ent from that held by rabbinic Judaism.
15. Helen Freeman, 'Chochmah and Wholeness', in Sybil Sheridan (ed.),
    Hear Our Voice (n. 10)
16. Abudarham, Section II, Blessings before the Mitzvot, cited in Getzel
    Ellison Halshah, *vHaMitzvot, Woman and the Commandments*,
    Vol. 1, World Zionist Organization, Jerusalem 1986, 40.

Discovering Hannah: Women's Rituals in Second-Century Palestine

1. I Samuel 1.10ff.
2. Berachot 31a.
3. For an example of this see the *tehine* of Sarah bat Tovim in Sondra
   Henry and Emily Taitz, *Written out of History*, New York: Biblio
   Press 1990, 192.
4. Mishnah Shabbat 2.6.
5. Judith Romney Wegner, *Chattel or Person?*, 155.
6. Mishnah Kiddushin 1.7.
7. Based on Leviticus 24.1–4.
8. Sondra Hendry and Emily Taitz, *Written out of History* (n.3), 192.
9. Women's testimony was only accepted in the case of a man who was
   presumed dead or regarding an incident that took place where only
   women were present, cf. Mishnah Yebamoth 15.4; Mishnah
   Shevuoth 4.1.
10. Genesis 35.17–20.
11. I Samuel 4.19–20.
12. See the pictorial record on the Arch of Titus in Rome.
13. See for example Amanda Golby, 'Women and the New Moon', in
    Sybil Sheridan (ed.), *Hear Our Voice*, SCM Press 1994. All we know
    of the once-popular women's Rosh Hodesh ceremonies is what has
    been written down by men.

The Little Boy Who Did Not Know How To Ask

1. *Passover Haggadah*, Union of Liberal and Progressive Synagogues 1981, 9.
2. Exodus 13.8.
3. The standard text of the *Mah Nishtanah* can be found in the *Haggadah*. The opening formula is usually translated 'Why is this night different from all other nights?'.

How To Pray When You Can't Pray

1. The use of the term 'God' can be problematic, especially for women for whom it conjures up an image of masculine power. But it is still commonly used in English translations and can embrace a variety of images of the Divine. It is not the main purpose of this chapter to address the language of prayer, so God will be used as a shorthand term, though we are aware of the problems it may pose.
2. E.Kübler-Ross, *On Death and Dying*, Macmillan 1969.
3. E.M. Umansky and D. Achron (eds), *Four Centuries of Women's Spirituality*, Boston: Beacon Press 1992, 52, based on the prologue to Lamentations Rabba XXIV.
4. Ibid., 221–2.
5. Jewish study is in any case often considered in rabbinic literature to be equivalent to prayer, both as a way of fulfilling one's duty and as a way of approaching God. Both are *avodah*, service of God (e.g. C. Montefiore and H. Loewe, eds, *Rabbinic Anthology*, New York: Schocken Books 1974, 186–7).
6. Kübler-Ross, *On Death and Dying* (n.1), 100.
7. Umansky and Achron (eds), *Four Centuries of Women's Spirituality* (n.2), 147.

Simhat B'rit M'ugelet: Rejoicing in Becoming Round: A Pregnancy Ritual

1. Tikva Frymer-Kensky, *Motherprayer. The Pregnant Woman's Spiritual Companion*, New York: Riverhead Books 1995, 94.
2. Ibid., 59.
3. Ibid., 72.
4. Ceremonies Sampler, San Diego Women's Continuing Education, San Diego, CA, 16–17.
5. Anita Diamant, *The Jewish Baby Book*, 33.
6. Frymer-Kensky, *Motherprayer. The Pregnant Woman's Spiritual Companion* (n.1), 96.
7. Ibid., 64.

At the Moment of Birth

1. From Psalm 8.
2. Genesis 1.27.
3. Isaiah 44.24.
4. From Babylonian Talmud Niddah 31a.

Simhat Bat: *Welcoming a Daughter*

1. Babylonian Talmud Megillah 14a.

Responding to the Cry: Reactions to Childlessness

1. The passages chosen for the readings and anthology have been collected and created by the Rosh Hodesh group of Southgate and District Reform Synagogue for their book on the loss of a baby called *Another Kind of Weeping*.
2. Words and music A. Hirshfield.
3. Dee Eimer, Lorna Jacobs and Jacqueline Tabick worked together on compiling this service.

A Ritual for the Termination of a Pregnancy

1. The following quotations are used: Genesis 25.22; Genesis 18.14; Genesis 30.6; Psalm 13.4; I Samuel 1.15; I Samuel 1.17.
2. II Samuel 12.16ff.
3. Freely taken from I Kings 9.3–13.
4. The following psalms are used to create this prayer: Psalms 31; 71; 139; 130; 13; 17.
5. Psalm 18.29; Psalm 31.
6. Bentsh Gomel, see *Singer's Prayer Book* and others.
7. *Forms of Prayer*, Reform Synagogues of Great Britain, 1997, 295–6.
8. Quotations taken from Psalm 30 and Psalm 1.3.

On the Breakdown of a Relationship

1. Blessing before the *Sh'ma*, Siddur Lev Hadash, 14.
2. The attribution comes from Marcia Falk, *The Book of Blessings*, HarperCollins 1996.
3. Ibid., 272.
4. Words of Hillel in Mishnah Abot 1.14.

A Rabbi's Experience of Illness

1. Each Shabbat takes its title from the first principal word of the Torah portion read that week.

Beginning a Religious Response to Mastectomy

1. Adapted from Jeremiah 4.31, 19–22, 23–26.
2. Adapted from Jeremiah 15.9
3. Adapted from Psalm 143.9–12.

Healing

1. My thanks to The National Centre for Jewish Healing, 9 East 69th Street, New York 10021.

Acknowledgments

We are grateful to Penguin Books Ltd for permission to quote Marge Piercy's 'A Strong Woman', which appears in her *The Eight Chambers of the Heart*, 1995; also to Riverhead Books, New York, for permission to quote from Tikva Frymer-Kensky, *Motherprayer. The Pregnant Woman's Spiritual Companion*, 1995. Also to Debbie Friedman, for her song *Likhi Lakh*.

We have done our best to identify and acknowledge copyright material; if we have failed in any way we apologize to those concerned and will endeavour to rectify the matter promptly.

Glossary

Afikomen
The piece of matzah broken off during the seder ceremony, and hidden, before being the last thing to be eaten that night.

Agunah
A woman whose husband has not released her from the marriage under Jewish law, and who therefore is unable to marry again.

Aleinu
Prayer proclaiming God as Sovereign over all humankind. It is recited as the closing prayer of the three statutory daily services.

Asher yatzar
A prayer in the morning service: 'Blessed are You, Adonai, our God and King of the Universe, Who has formed the human being with wisdom...'

Avot or *Pirkei Avot*
Tractate in the Mishnah which records sayings by the teachers of the Hellenistic and Roman periods.

Bar/Bat Mitzvah
Usually describes the ceremony of religious majority, when the child is called to the reading of the Torah during the synagogue service. Also describes the state of coming of age.

Bimah
The raised platform in the synagogue from which the service is led.

B'rakhah/b'rakhot
'Blessing/blessings' - in Judaism blessings are said before many actions, setting them into a context of 'mitzvah' – commandment.

B'rit Milah
'Covenant of circumcision'.

Beit Din
A religious court consisting of three scholars of Jewish law.

Dreidel
The spinning top used at Hanukkah to play a gambling game.

Get
The document of divorce, given by the husband and accepted by the wife.

Haggadah/Haggadot
The book used to tell the story of the exodus from Egypt during the *Seder* services of Passover.

Halakhah/halakhic
The word *halakhah* is used to denote law, guidance and traditional practice. '*Halakhic*' therefore has come to mean 'legal' or 'with the authority of tradition'.

Hanukkah
The festival which commemorates the rededication of the Temple in 165 BCE, after the Maccabean revolt.

Haroset
A mixture of nuts and fruit, used at the Passover *Seder* as a symbol of the mortar that the Israelite slaves used to make bricks from in Egypt.

Havdalah
The ritual marking the end of the sabbath.

Huppah
The canopy held over the bride and groom's head as they marry. Also used to mean the wedding ceremony.

Kaddish
A prayer which glorifies and praises God. Mourners recite it during the period of mourning, and on the anniversary of the death.

Kavvanah
The concentration and intention of the individual at prayer.

K'dushah
The third paragraph of the *T'fillah*, the major prayer in the statutory service. The *k'dushah* declaims the holiness of God.

K'tubah/k'tubot
The marriage document(s).

Kiddush
The sanctification of sabbaths and holy days, recited over wine.

Mah Nishtanah
A passage from the *Haggadah* commonly recited by the youngest member present, it asks four questions about why this night (Passover night) is different from all other nights.

Mah Tovu
A prayer recited at the beginning of the service.

Matzah
The unleavened bread eaten during Passover.

M'gillah
The scroll of the Book of Esther, read at Purim.

M'norah
The eight-branched candlestick lit at Hanukkah.

Mikveh (plural *mikva'ot*)
The pool of living waters which are used for ritual immersion.

Midrash
Expositional and homiletic literature which explains the biblical text in many different ways.

Mi She'beirakh
An opening formula for invoking the divine blessing on others, for example when they are called to the reading of the Torah.

Mitzvah/mitzvot
'Commandment(s)', technically one of the 613 specific commands found in Bible. Also used to describe ethical action and acts of kindness.

Motza'ey Shabbat
'The going out of the sabbath'. Also refers to Saturday evening.

Niggun
A wordless prayer bound up with repeating a gently insistent tone.

N'shamah y'terah
'Extra soul' : tradition has it that we are given an extra soul which leaves us at the end of shabbat.

Pesah
Passover: the eight-day springtime festival during which Jews commemorate the exodus from Egypt.

P'tihah
'Opening': the term for the beginning formula of a prayer or blessing.

Rodef
'Pursuer'. The biblical term used for someone who is pursuing another to take his/her life. Later becomes a category in rabbinic law.

Rosh Hodesh
'New month': the day after the crescent of new moon was first sighted was treated as a festival in ancient Israel.

Seder
'Order': the service celebrated in the home on the first two nights of Passover.

Shabbat
'Sabbath': the period from dusk on Friday night to darkness on Saturday night.

Sh'loshim
'Thirty': the thirty days of full mourning following the funeral.

Sh'monah Esreh
Also known as the *T'fillah* or *Amidah* prayer. It is the central prayer of each statutory service and is read standing.

Sheol
The place of silence into which the dead are said to descend.

Sheva B'rakhot
The seven blessings which are said as part of the marriage service, and also recited at meals during the seven days following the wedding.

Shivah
'Seven': the seven days of intense mourning following the funeral. The family 'sit *shivah*' while the community supports them with visiting, food, company etc.

Siddur
The daily and sabbath prayer book.

Sefer Torah
The handwritten scroll containing the five books of Moses, read in the synagogue on Mondays, Thursdays, Saturdays, Rosh Hodesh and Festivals.

Sukkot
Feast of tabernacles: eight-day autumn festival commemorating the wanderings of the children of Israel in the wilderness when they lived in booths.

Tallit
The shawl used during morning prayer.

Talmud
Collection of 63 tractates containing laws, narratives, history, allegory, prayers, ethics, discussion on philosophical and theological ideas, etc.

Tehine/tehines
Devotional prayers and private meditations composed as additions to the statutory prayers.

T'fillah
Prayer. The *T'fillah par excellence* is the *Amidah*.

T'fillin
Phylacteries. They consist of two cases containing parchment scrolls upon which are written biblical verses. They are placed on the forehead, and the arm during weekday morning prayer, as a visible reminder to study and do the word of God.

T'villah
The immersion in the ritual bath (*mikveh*).

Tetragrammaton
The four letter name of God, Yod Hay Vav Hay. Never spoken out loud.

Tzitzit
The fringes on a four cornered garment to remind the wearer of the presence of God and the commandments incumbent on him/her.

Unterfuehren
Yiddish for the people who accompany the groom to the *huppah*.

Yahrzeit
The anniversary of a death.

Yihud
The period of time immediately after the wedding ceremony when the bride and groom fulfil the requirement of being alone together.

Yizkor
The service of memorial, conducted on Yom Kippur and the last day of the festivals of Pesah, Sukkot and Shavuot.

Notes on Contributors

Hadassah Davis is rabbi to the Bristol and West Progressive Jewish Congregation and is a trainee psychotherapist. She has had articles published on conversion; aspects of fertility in medical ethics; and the role of the Wannsee Conference in the 'final solution'. She enjoys Jewish meditation, dabbling with pastels, and glass painting, but her passionate love, apart from her husband, is canals and narrowboating.

Helen Freeman was a speech therapist with a particular interest in stammering and voice disorders. She was ordained in 1990 as a rabbi and served the Liberal Jewish Synagogue before becoming associate rabbi at West London Synagogue. She has continued her training with courses at the Westminster Pastoral Foundation, London Marriage Guidance and the Independent Group of Analytical Psychologists. She is married to Rabbi David Freeman.

Amanda Golby was rabbi of the Southport New Synagogue and Nottingham Progressive Synagogue. A former librarian, she is interested in liturgy and the development of spirituality.

Harriett Goldenberg is a chartered counselling psychologist and Existential Psychotherapist in private practice, and on the visiting faculty of the School of Psychotherapy and Counselling, Regent's College. She is a former Chair of RSGB/ULPS Social Action.

Margaret Jacobi is the rabbi of Birmingham Progressive Synagogue. She studied medicine at Birmingham University and then obtained a PhD in physiology. She draws on her previous experience by maintaining an interest in medical ethics and Talmudic medicine and has publications in both fields.

Miri Lawrence trained at Leo Baeck College, and was rabbi at Ealing Liberal Synagogue for four years. Currently she is devoted to bringing up her two small children, especially in the light of her son's special needs, and the impact this also has on her daughter. She is finding out as much as she can about autism and is developing ways of teaching autistic children, with special reference to teaching Judaism.

Rachel Montagu was educated at Newnham College, Cambridge, Leo Baeck College, London and Machon Pardes Jerusalem. She teaches for a number of institutions including Allen Hall (Biblical Hebrew) and Birkbeck College (Biblical Hebrew and Hebrew Bible) and Edgware Reform Synagogue (GCSE Jewish Studies).

Marcia R. Plumb was born and raised in Houston, Texas. She was ordained at Hebrew Union College-Jewish Institute of Religion in New York. She has lived in London since 1990. She is a co-founder of two national Jewish women's organizations and a contributor to *Hear Our Voice*, the first volume of essays from women rabbis published by SCM Press. She has been a congregational rabbi and also specializes in women's studies, rituals and liturgy. She is married to Michael Shire, and is the proud mother of Anya.

Sylvia Rothschild is rabbi of the Bromley and District Reform Synagogue. Currently co-chair of the Assembly of Rabbis, she has written on spiritual approaches to death and dying, new liturgies, and women and illness. Married with two children, her other activities include medical ethics, racial equality and refugee issues.

Elizabeth Tikvah Sarah, a graduate of LSE and Leo Baeck College, is rabbi of Leicester Progressive Jewish Congregation and a lecturer at Leo Baeck College (Hebrew; Spirituality), where she also chairs the Rabbinic In-Service Training Team. A co-editor of *Hochmah,* she has edited three books, contributed three dozen articles and several poems to various anthologies and journals and is writing *Teasing Texts and Telling Tales. A Jewish Feminist Exploration of Torah* (SCM Press 2001).

Sybil Sheridan is rabbi of the Thames Valley Progressive Jewish Community in Reading and lectures in Bible, Life Cycle and Festivals at the Leo Baeck College. Editor of *Hear our Voice: Women Rabbis tell their Stories* (SCM Press 1994), she has contributed articles to various books on Judaism and Biblical studies.

Sheila Shulman was born in New York City in 1936, but she has lived in London since 1970. Ordained at Leo Baeck College in 1989, Sheila is rabbi of Beit KIal Yisrael (North Kensington Reform Synagogue) and associate rabbi of Finchley Reform Synagogue. She is a lecturer in theology and philosophy at the Leo Baeck College.

Jacqueline Tabick was the first woman to be ordained as a rabbi in the UK. She is rabbi of the North West Surrey Synagogue and vice-chair of the World Congress of Faiths.

Lee Wax was ordained in 1994 at the Leo Baeck College, having formerly been a primary school teacher and then a senior Jewish educator. She has been rabbi of Sukkat Shalom Synagogue in east London and is associate rabbi at the North Western Reform Synagogue in Golders Green. She is married to Dr John Launer and is the mother of twins Ruth and David.

Alexandra Wright is the rabbi of Radlett and Bushey Reform Synagogue in Hertfordshire. She has taught Classical Hebrew at Leo Baeck College and has contributed articles on Judaism and on feminist theology to various books and journals. She

worked on the editorial committee for the new Liberal Jewish
Prayer book, *Siddur Lev Hadash*. She is married and has two
children.